Elizabeth May is an environmentalist, writer, activist, and lawyer. She is the author of seven books and the recipient of numerous awards, including being named an Officer of the Order of Canada. Since her 2006 election as leader of the Green Party of Canada, she has led the party to an unprecedented level of support among Canadians. May and her daughter, Victoria Cate, divide their time between Ottawa and New Glasgow, Nova Scotia.

Author photograph: Langston James Goree VI

Losing Confidence

Also by

ELIZABETH MAY

Budworm Battles: The Fight to Stop the Aerial Insecticide
Spraying of the Forests of Eastern Canada

Paradise Won: The Struggle to Save South Moresby

At the Cutting Edge: The Crisis in Canada's Forests

Frederick Street: Life and Death on Canada's Love Canal
(with Maude Barlow)

How to Save the World in Your Spare Time

Global Warming for Dummies (with Zoë Caron)

Losing Confidence

*Power, Politics, and the Crisis
in Canadian Democracy*

ELIZABETH

MAY

*For Leonardo,
Many thanks for your
support!*

[signature]

McCLELLAND & STEWART

LIBRARY AND ARCHIVES CANADA CATALOGUING IN PUBLICATION

May, Elizabeth
Losing confidence : power, politics and the crisis in
Canadian democracy / Elizabeth May.

ISBN 978-0-7710-5760-1

1. Canada – Politics and government – 2006-. 2. Canada – Politics and
government – 2006- – Citizen participation. I. Title.

FC640.M33 2009   971.07'3   C2009-901209-X

We acknowledge the financial support of the Government of Canada
through the Book Publishing Industry Development Program and that
of the Government of Ontario through the Ontario Media Development
Corporation's Ontario Book Initiative. We further acknowledge the
support of the Canada Council for the Arts and the Ontario Arts Council
for our publishing program.

Printed and bound in Canada

ANCIENT FOREST
FRIENDLY

This book is printed on acid-paper that is 100% recycled,
ancient-forest friendly (40% post-consumer recycled).

McClelland & Stewart Ltd.
75 Sherbourne Street
Toronto, Ontario
M5A 2P9
www.mcclelland.com

1 2 3 4 5   13 12 11 10 09

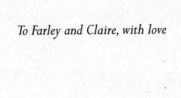

To Farley and Claire, with love

CONTENTS

Introduction

IT WAS IN EARLY MAY 2006 that I first watched *An Inconvenient Truth,* the now famous Oscar-winning documentary about the climate crisis. The Sierra Club of Canada had organized an advance screening in Toronto to which media, politicians, and various opinion leaders had been invited. Al Gore was there to make his pitch for a word-of-mouth movement to increase attention for the documentary.

I was on my way out of my role as executive director of Sierra Club of Canada. After seventeen years, I had given notice a few months earlier, and although most of my staff did not know it, I had decided to toss my hat in the ring for the leadership of the Green Party of Canada. So, while I served as MC as Al Gore fielded questions, I was on the verge of moving in the opposite direction. He had left politics and embraced a life as an environmental advocate, and I was preparing to do the reverse.

A question was posed to Gore at that session and his answer stayed with me and has shaped my thinking over the last few years. In talking about the climate crisis, Gore said that it was one aspect of the crisis in Western democracies. He mentioned that the democracy crisis in Canada did not seem as extreme as in the U.S. (a point that needed no explanation given the theft of the U.S. election in 2000), but that every modern democracy was in crisis. And he believed that without fully functioning democracies, we could not escape the worst outcomes of global warming.

I had come to the same conclusion. We had just emerged from a federal election in which the old-line party I had once thought cared most about the climate crisis, the NDP, took pains to avoid climate change as an issue. Just two years before, the NDP had highlighted the threat. NDP television ads in the 2004 campaign showcased Jack Layton calling for real action on the environment as he posed next to a gentle stream. Then NDP strategists watched as Paul Martin blitzed from coast to coast calling for NDP voters to vote Liberal to stop Harper, describing the two parties as coming from "the same wellspring." It worked and Martin squeaked back in with a minority government. By fall of 2005, Jack Layton had decided he was not content with forcing changes to the minority government's budget. In a meeting with other opposition leaders, he struck a deal to bring down the Paul Martin government on November 28, 2005, unless Martin agreed to trigger an election and end his government early in the New Year.

It was an audacious threat of questionable constitutionality. What the news media missed, as they focused on whether Canadians would stand for an election over Christmas, was the most galling element of the Harper-Layton and Duceppe gambit; November 28 was the opening day of the most important global climate negotiations in history. The 11th Conference of the Parties (COP) to the UN Framework Convention on Climate Change was the first session to take place following the February 2005 enactment of the Kyoto Protocol. Kyoto had been signed in 1997 and the expectation was that the ratification process would have concluded by 2000. Instead, Kyoto was not binding international law until 2005. The agenda for COP 11 was daunting and urgent. As the first meeting of ratifying parties under Kyoto, the conference had to establish Kyoto's operations. At the same time, within the first phase of the agreement, negotiators had to begin work on the next phase of action. Worse yet, Canada was the host for those negotiations, set to take place in Montreal. With Canada's government falling on the opening day, the whole process could be derailed. The president of the COP was, under the UN terms of hosting, the environment minister from the host country, Stéphane Dion.

Environmentalists from around the world were horrified. Climate Action Network international activists had met in Montreal in September to plan. The odds were against a successful negotiation. The Bush administration did not support Kyoto and the role of Canada as host was critical. If Dion was in an election, could he perform his duties? He had spent much of the previous year in shuttle diplomacy, getting to know the lead ministers from around the world in order to broker a deal more effectively. I remember phoning Jack Layton to beg him not to bring down the government on the opening day of the climate conference. I had known and liked Jack since he was on Toronto City Council. He had been enormously helpful, volunteering as an auctioneer in local Sierra Club events. He told me when he ran for leader of the NDP that he was only seeking a role in federal politics to deal with the climate crisis. I had believed him. As he threatened to sabotage the most important global climate negotiations in history, I recall leaving a message on his cellphone: "How will you look at yourself in the mirror if you do this?" We spoke a few times. He was angry that Sierra Club had issued a press release saying, "There's more at stake than Christmas" and highlighting the threat to the Montreal talks. I had begged him to wait for a money vote in the House already scheduled for December 8. It was to no avail.

Thankfully, Dion told the world immediately after the government fell that he now worked for the United Nations. He said he would resume his life as a Canadian politician on December 10, when the meeting was over.

Incredibly, he steered the meetings to the high-water mark of possible objectives, across every issue. I may never have had a happier moment than when the meetings concluded on December 11 at 6:17 in the morning after round-the-clock negotiations. Dion brought down the gavel on the most aggressive possible actions to advance limits in the next commitment period, set to begin in 2013. I may never have been as devastated as when Stephen Harper was elected, knowing he would do whatever he could to stop progress in reducing greenhouse gases.

What we didn't see as a further disaster in bringing down the government on November 28 was that it effectively rendered the Montreal negotiations invisible to the Canadian public. The media was off on the typical brainless pursuit of Canadian election as horserace. Policy and science, particularly UN discussions of the climate crisis, were not going to be covered in an election campaign.

It is only with hindsight that I have come to believe that the climate negotiations were not merely collateral damage to the incidental timing of November 28. I now believe that Harper and Layton had a shared desire to pull the plug before the Martin government had a chance to look good on the world stage. I think it is extremely likely, given the way Layton downplayed the climate threat in 2006, that a conscious decision was made by NDP strategists. They had to make sure the key issue remained Liberal corruption for the NDP to avoid losing votes to the Liberals. If voters started noticing that Harper was against Kyoto, and that the Liberals finally had a (reasonable if not excellent) plan, votes would shift to the Liberals again. Both Harper and Layton adopted the adage "The enemy of my enemy is my friend." For very different reasons, neither one wanted Kyoto to be an election issue.

Jack Layton steadfastly avoided pointing out that the Conservatives opposed living up to Kyoto. The NDP feared prompting their soft vote going Liberal to block a Conservative win. So the issue of climate did not figure in the election. Neither did foreign policy. The issue of the day was not the one that would threaten future generations or claim Canadian lives in Afghanistan. Both the Conservatives and the NDP, with lots of help from a supine media, decided the critical issue was the Sponsorship Scandal. The most outraged denunciations of that misadventure had come from the Liberal Leader Paul Martin, so arguing about how bad the Sponsorship Scandal really was was like shooting fish in a barrel. Nevertheless, attack ads from the NDP and Conservatives piled on the abuse with the clear implication that any future Liberal government would be corrupt to its foundations. Meanwhile the Liberals put forward their own attack ads with a somber voice over about the worst possible excesses of Mr. Harper and his "secret agenda." Our elections seemed to be going the way of those in the U.S.– politics as a form of warfare.

Additionally, we were in an election in which the turning point in the fortunes of the front-running parties would be a bizarre and unprecedented intervention by the state police. Yet no one seemed to be talking about it. Later I was convinced that the Conservative minority of Stephen Harper had been elected by accident. Forty per cent of the 36 percent who voted Conservative said they had done so to punish the Liberals. While overall voter turn out improved only slightly over the 2004 historic lows, with only 64.7 percent of Canadians voting. Meanwhile some commentators noted with dismay that it was only due to the archaic "first past the post" system, a method of elections developed 1,100 years ago, that so many votes had not helped their party of choice. The House ended up not reflecting the will of the people as expressed through their votes.

So, it was hard to argue with the notion that democracy in Canada was in crisis. In entering politics, I felt that I could bring something different to the situation. At least, if I succeeded in becoming leader of the Green Party, I could draw attention to critical issues in the next election campaign. I wanted to identify what was wrong with Canadian politics: the marketing and selling of politicians like consumer goods; the failure to raise important issues and do so in respectful discourse. I wanted to help change the culture of politics from a confrontational and competitive field to one where greater cooperation and respect would be possible. If I could, I wanted to end the sports metaphors for politics as a "game" and see it for what it is and must be: the exercise by a free and responsible people of the democratic right to choose their own future.

Since then, the crisis has intensified. For the first time in Canadian political life, attack ads have been launched outside an election cycle. The Conservative "Not a Leader" tag line for Stéphane Dion was drummed into voters' heads in January 2007 – mere weeks after Stéphane Dion won the Liberal leadership.

The increasing prominence of a presidential-style prime minister is steadily denigrating the traditions and institutions of Canadian democracy. Although the trend toward expanding prime ministerial powers began under Prime Minister Trudeau, the exercise of total control under Stephen Harper is unlike anything in Canadian tradition. The House of Commons has experienced an unprecedented increase of filibusters to block work in that chamber – instigated by Conservative MPs following a handbook produced by the PMO to ensure unfavourable witnesses could not speak in committees and unwanted bills could not pass in the House.

Question Period has sunk to the lowest levels of rudeness and incivility in living memory. Loud rounds of booing from government benches greet certain opposition members before they can even form a question. And the Speaker fails to rein them in. Every question to the prime minister is treated as an excuse to attack the questioner — or someone else. Once from my perch in the front row of the diplomatic gallery, I watched the leader of the official opposition ask about treatment of Afghan prisoners. The prime minister used this question to attack me, distorting a comment I had made on an unrelated subject beyond recognition. Politics has been referred to as a "blood sport." It is rapidly becoming a take-no-prisoners war — both in and out of elections.

Public policy is no longer being developed through a process of consensus reflecting the public will. Nor is it being developed based on what the country needs in response to issues of concern — whether it's the economic downturn borne of the credit crisis, the growing gap between the rich and the poor, the persistent weaknesses in our health care system, or the environmental crisis. Issues are dealt with solely with an eye on the next election. Policies are not designed with the broad public interest in mind, but with a narrow segmentation of Canadian voter attitudes, sliced and diced down to a level of manipulation that can win seats, if not the hearts and minds of the majority. The precision of targeted bad policy with the aim of winning seats is being brought to the level of high art under the current government.

We are increasingly observing all the levers of power of government — and governance — being appropriated from even a semblance of serving the public good in order to serve the Conservative Party's fortunes in the next election.

The problem is that so few people seem to remember it was not always like this.

Jane Jacobs commented on this aspect of modern society in her last book, *Dark Age Ahead*. As pillars of our civilization crumble, Jacobs noted, we suffer from a collective amnesia. We seem to readjust rapidly without noticing what is being lost.

A full, free, and functioning democracy is not something we should lose without a fight. We must not be driven by fear or seduced by creature comforts into allowing democracy to slip between our fingers.

The first thing we must do is to remind ourselves of our system of government. We live in a parliamentary democracy. I don't know that it can be said that our young people have forgotten as much as that (through the failures of our educational system, which Jacobs also decried) they were never taught in a way that conveyed any relevance to them.

We did not rebel against King George III. Canada's founding fathers did not sign on to the Declaration of Independence to reject constitutional monarchy. We do not live in a governmental system of separation of powers – of a legislative branch, an executive branch and a judiciary. By pointing this out, I intend no criticism of the U.S. system. Three of my ancestors signed the Declaration of Independence. It's just that any system of government has its pluses and minuses and it's important to understand the system of government you do live under so that you can protect it.

The creation of a "presidential" prime minister, the increasing weakness of any real Cabinet system, and the impotence of members of Parliament, all point to a serious risk for the health of our democracy.

My love of parliamentary democracy started late in life. I grew up in the United States. My parents moved the whole family to Cape Breton Island in the early 1970s. I had had a very political childhood in the States. I knew senators and congressmen. I had helped my mother collect names on petitions and conduct election campaigns to support Democrats opposed to the continuation of the war in Vietnam. At fourteen, I had been tear-gassed in Chicago at the 1968 Democratic Convention and watched billy-club-wielding cops and National Guard troops with barbed wire strung across the front of their jeeps clear the city parks of people. That experience gave me a profound sense of how fragile human rights and democracy really are.

Once in Canada, I wanted to learn everything about how the system of government worked. My dad had grown up in England so he understood how parliamentary democracy worked. I was enormously proud when I took my oath of Canadian citizenship, having overprepared for the exam. Due to family financial reverses I had not gone to university, but was waitressing and cooking in our family business. When the tourists were gone, in the winter months, I volunteered in local campaigns to prevent aerial insecticide spraying.

I can vividly recall being dismayed by the first Canadian attack ad I ever saw on television. It was in the early days of the 1979–80 election. I can now only recall the hands moving on a chess board, but the content was an attack on Joe Clark paid for by the Liberals. Even though it was meek and mild compared to today's attack ads, I hated it. It propelled me to start a small political effort that we called the "small party" to run candidates raising environmental issues. We ran thirteen candidates in six provinces. I ran against Allan J. MacEachen, a man I truly admired for his social policy and for his acumen as a great parliamentarian. He just didn't notice environmental issues. They were not in his generation's frame of reference. Over time some of those who had joined the "small party" effort kept that idea of a fledgling party alive. By 1983 the "small party" had become the Green Party of Canada.

My next major learning curve in understanding Canadian democracy was in 1986 when I was recruited by the federal minister of environment. Tom McMillan was a young and keen Progressive Conservative MP from Prince Edward Island. He was determined to turn the Mulroney government into one with a good environmental record. It was certainly audacious to invite a non-Conservative environmental lawyer and activist to advise on policy from within the minister's political staff. He announced my appointment and was then shocked to find that Nova Scotia Conservatives were in an uproar. He managed to weather that storm, keeping me away from any partisan aspects of his office, and allowing me to concentrate on policy.

In the two years I worked in his office I learned an enormous amount about how government can work in the public interest. On issue after issue, from creating national parks to negotiating the Montreal Protocol to protect the ozone layer, Tom McMillan had a pan-partisan approach. He would regularly send me to brief the opposition environment critics.

When I watch the House and the behaviour of parliamentarians today I am all the sadder because I know personally how much better it can be. In the summer of 1987, I was in the public gallery for the free vote on capital punishment. Those who wanted Canada to remain a civilized society that forbade state murder had worked tirelessly across party lines to have the vote succeed.

Try to imagine that now. There is no cooperation. There is no effort at consensus. The House has become toxic through excessive partisanship and collective amnesia has wiped away the sure knowledge that it does not have to be like this.

If Canadians heard about a country where a handful of people controlled all the news media, where the state police could deliberately interfere in an election to settle a personal score for the head cop, where the prime minister enjoyed excessive power, we would justly picture a Third World nation that languishes behind modern democracies. It is very unlikely we would see ourselves in that description.

Despite the parliamentary crisis of November 2008, Canadians are not particularly aware that the essence of our democracy is at risk. The essential elements of a functional democracy are a free and independent media, a well-informed and engaged electorate, and high levels of participation on voting day.

We could have greater levels of participation in elections. We need to set aside aggressive, combative politics to allow the public to believe there are people and policies worth voting for. We could reform our voting system to allow proportional representation. We could jolt our news media out of their stupor to actually cover issues and solutions, and not allow the political process to be further dumbed down through inane commentary masquerading as journalism. We could engage in a respectful discourse. And, fundamentally, we could reverse the dangerous trends that are allowing our parliamentary democracy to warp into the worst of all worlds – an imperial prime ministerial rule in the absence of the checks and balances placed on U.S. presidential powers.

Our democracy is precious. It is worth fighting for.

Chapter 1

The Degradation of
Canadian Parliamentary Democracy

TO UNDERSTAND THE DANGEROUS trends affecting Canadian parliamentary democracy, we need to revisit how it was supposed to work. We need to understand its history.

The early concepts of democracy were born in a far different time and culture. In the city states of Ancient Greece, where women and slaves had no status, the idea of free men making decisions that affected their lives was new and pure. As Pericles said of Athenians, "A man who does not participate in the city we do not think lives at all."[1]

I participate, therefore I am.

Canadian parliamentary democracy comes from Britain. On the field at Runnymede in 1215, King John of England accepted limits on his authority through the Magna Carta. Those limits had to do with the rights of a free man not to be deprived of the basics of life — his property, his liberty — through the whim of a monarch. The Magna Carta said that the king was not the law, nor above the law. A loose consultation with a council of lords and peers was required before the monarch could act. Over time this evolved into an actual parliament composed of a House of Commoners and a House of Lords. By the fourteenth century, the king was asking the commoners to elect a Speaker so that he could consult with an elected spokesman. It was up to those common men if they met in advance to tell the Speaker what he should tell the king.[2] The historical process that evolved into parliamentary democracy had begun.

The rise of the middle class, driven by the burgeoning commercial wool trade, elevated the role of the common man, and Parliament became more formalized under the rule of the Tudors. Queen Elizabeth I was adept at handling Parliament: proper consultation, respectful manipulation.

It was not until the Industrial Revolution that the role of the monarch became clearly ceremonial and that of elected members of Parliament grew in importance. In Britain, the *Reform Act* of 1832 brought about a shift in which the middle class gained more power and there was a new balance between urban and rural districts. Gradually, elected members grew more numerous and their connection to local voters more tenuous. Candidates began to campaign by expressing to voters their hopes of working closely with a particular person – someone with the natural characteristics of leadership. Factions had been a feature of political life since the seventeenth century, when *Whig* and

Tory were invented as pejorative terms. In the late 1800s, candidates who wished to be associated with Disraeli ran against those who wanted to work with Gladstone, and the Whigs and the Tories had evolved into the English Liberal and Conservative parties.

If I were inventing democracy from scratch I would not have invented political parties. In their current form, at their worst they represent an impediment to independent thought. Mindless partisanship insists on a team mentality. My team versus your team — at all times and in all circumstances. Political parties began innocently enough, but they are hardly an integral part of the business of democracy. The party system elevates the "leader" above the collective members of Parliament. And it shifts the focus of elections from who is the best candidate in a local area to who might be the best prime minister. In 1861 when John Stuart Mill wrote *Considerations on Representative Government,* he did not even mention their existence. Political parties are not referred to in the Canadian Constitution, and until the 1960s, ballots did not identify to which political party a candidate belonged.[3] Canadians voted for individuals. The role of parties was initially so minor that MPs moved from allegiance to allegiance. Sir John A. Macdonald referred to MPs as "loose fish."[4] Like many fish these days, independent-minded MPs are an endangered species.

In today's democracy, political parties have become a dominant part of the landscape. In fact, the word *politics* conjures up nothing as much as the partisan contest between the differing ideologies (increasingly called "brands") of various parties. The distortion of democracy due to the rise of organized political parties is merely part of our current crisis.

By the twentieth century the limited role of the monarch was firmly established and the essentials of parliamentary democracy were clear. Elected members had a great deal of autonomy, but did work within a party system. The notion of the "prime minister" was initially "first among equals." The prime minister was both the leader of the party that had gained the most seats (if not the most votes) and the head of the government.

The prime minister's role was far different from that of the U.S. president. The American founding fathers were concerned more with the abuse of power than with the exercise of it. They separated the executive function from the legislative and judiciary functions. Working under a constitution born of idealism, they hoped to put brakes on the ruthless exercise of power through the distribution of that power among different bodies. The U.S. president is head of the executive powers of the government. However, the House of Representatives and the Senate (which make up Congress) can thwart the president on many matters, as can the judiciary. In fact, in the early years of the United States, Thomas Jefferson was probably more vexed by the chief justice of the Supreme Court, John Marshall, than by the elected members of the Congress. The president, especially in the initial conception of the American system of government, had virtually no unilateral powers. All of his actions required legislative approval.

Things are quite different in a constitutional monarchy like Canada. In a parliamentary democracy, Parliament has powers that are both executive and legislative. The Canadian system essentially vested both executive and legislative powers in the same body — Parliament, composed of the House of Commons and the Senate. In other words, historically in Canada we have a government made up of elected MPs, with the prime minister acting as the coordinator of the governmental work of the entire House of Commons. Meanwhile, the Senate fills the role of the British House of Lords. It reviews legislation and holds hearings on its own initiative. Lacking the legitimacy that comes from being elected, the Senate rarely interferes with the will of the House. But as the House and its legislative role have evolved in recent years, the prime minister now has control over both the executive and the legislative functions of government to an alarming extent.

Canadian parliamentary democracy might have chosen to evolve from the system of government practised by the Iroquois Confederacy. If one were looking for a geographical advantage for home-grown democracy, one couldn't improve on the example of the Haudenosaunee Confederacy on Turtle Island: 900 years of democracy, including a separation of powers with powerful balancing coming from the matriarchs of the society, presided over by a "Great Law of Peace." The American Revolutionaries took note of the civilized approach to governance of the Haudenosaunee, but our Canadian forefathers were steeped in a different tradition.

In his book *A Fair Country,* John Ralston Saul makes the case that Canada is a "Métis civilization."[5] While he acknowledges we have embraced the narrative of pre-dominant European colonial influences, he believes that in our bones we are influenced by the notions of fairness, cooperation, and community that are part and parcel of the indigenous civilization that predated European contact: "We are a people of Aboriginal inspiration organized around a concept of peace, fairness and good government."[6] The layering of the communitarian influences from Aboriginal culture may well have affected Canadian values, but the structure of our institutions owes more to the British parliamentary tradition.

As in Britain, the queen is our head of state, with the governor general acting as the queen's representative. The position is largely ceremonial but it serves a useful purpose in avoiding the raising up of an elected official, along with his family, to royal status. In the United States, presidential relatives become the "first family." Children and family pets are treated like royalty. It seems that in the absence of a hereditary monarchy, full of pomp and ceremony and tradition, even the most ostentatiously egalitarian of nations will invent a royal family.

In addition to the role of prime minister was the role of the Cabinet. In early British democracy, Cabinet ministers were appointed by the king. But in modern times, as issues became more complex and the governmental bureaucracy more daunting, the prime minister could seek to delegate some of the work of the House to one of the elected members of his party and (rarely) to an unelected member of the House of Lords or, in Canada, of the Senate. The Cabinet was initially quite small. Sir John A.'s Cabinet had a dozen members. In Mulroney's Cabinet, there were more than forty.

Even the Cabinet does not exist by name as a matter of law. It is not mentioned in the *Constitution Act* (1982) at all. What is named is the Privy Council of Canada. The anachronistically named Privy Council is an advisory group to the queen (through her representative, the governor general), and while it is primarily composed of the same people as the Cabinet, it performs a different function within a constitutional monarchy in a parliamentary democracy. The group of privy councillors is actually far larger than its operational element (the Cabinet). Under the *Constitution Act,* the Privy Council is appointed by the governor general. That is why the swearing in of a Cabinet happens in Rideau Hall, with the oath and pledge of secrecy administered by the governor general. Members of the

Privy Council are allowed access to the most top-secret of government information, under the *Security of Information Act*. Technically, anyone who has ever served as a Cabinet minister remains a member of the Privy Council forever. The designation "PC" after their name denotes that. Former prime minister Brian Mulroney broke with the tradition of limiting Privy Council membership to honour a number of distinguished Canadians on the occasion of Canada's 125th birthday. Mulroney appointed eighteen people, including media giant Conrad Black, artist Alex Colville, international diplomat and self-made millionaire Maurice Strong, Power Corp. chair Paul Desmarais, and Montreal businessman Charles Bronfman.[7] Despite the large group of Canadians who are technically part of the Privy Council, operationally it is restricted to current members of Cabinet. Decisions of the Cabinet have no status in law until sent as advice to the governor general, who returns them as minutes or Orders in Council passed by the "Governor General in Council."

The challenges of governing during the Second World War elevated the powers of Cabinet in relation to Parliament. British Prime Minister Winston Churchill set in motion a trend that appeared irreversible, and the same occurred in Canada. The Canadian Cabinet between 1939 and 1945 passed over 60,000 Orders in Council and 60,000 Treasury minutes. As Canadian academic and policy expert Donald Savoie points out, it would have been impossible for such a volume of decisions to be reviewed by Parliament: "The focus of activity and decision during the war had clearly shifted from Parliament to Cabinet and it would never shift back."[8]

Each Cabinet minister also had a great deal of independence, working in a committee system in which every opinion counted for something. For many years it could be said that Canada had an effective Cabinet system of government. However, that system has been steadily eroding as the power of prime minister has increased. And the surest indicator of the growth of the power of the prime minister is the expansion of the size and power of the Prime Minister's Office – or PMO, as it is generally known.

Back in 1928, a young Lester B. Pearson joined the civil service. He later recalled that "the Prime Minister's Office, including stenographers, file clerks, and messengers, could not have comprised much more than a dozen."[9]

The first prime minister to expand the powers of his office was Pierre Trudeau. Under Trudeau, the PMO grew by leaps and bounds. It expanded to over eighty people and has grown ever since. There was still a fully functional Cabinet with strong talent in the room. Trudeau started the practice (discontinued under Stephen Harper) of appointing a deputy prime minister, in his case the great parliamentarian Allan J. MacEachen. The deputy prime minister presided over the operations of the Privy Council Office (essentially the deputy minister function to the prime minister). The Privy Council Office (PCO) is the part of the government

23

system that oversees the decisions made by Cabinet and is headed by the country's most powerful civil servant, the Clerk of the Privy Council.

As the powers of the PMO grew, the relative role of Cabinet shrank — just as the role of the House had declined in the Second World War in preference to a larger Cabinet role. Canada's parliamentary government was in a steady trend toward greater centralization of power. Tom Kent, a distinguished Canadian who has made huge contributions to public policy in his various appointments, served as principal secretary to Prime Minister Pearson. Kent describes Pearson's government as "Canada's last *cabinet* government. That, not prime ministerial autocracy, was how Canada's parliamentary democracy had worked for the first hundred years."[10]

The growth in PMO control was also aided by the advent of politics on television. The PMO began to worry about the "optics" of government action. As Eddie Goldenberg, former chief of staff to Jean Chrétien, explained in his memoir, "Whether it is a good or bad story, there is no consistent story at all if you have more than two dozen Cabinet ministers all making announcements any time they see fit, about anything they want, without any planning or coordination."[11]

The expanded role of the PMO in serving a coordination function did not end the delegated authority of Cabinet ministers. Cabinet ministers under Mulroney,

Chrétien, and Martin did have a powerful role. Ministers made decisions within their mandate, gave speeches that set policy, and developed proposals to Cabinet.

John Turner served in both the Pearson and the Trudeau Cabinets. He bristled at the intrusions of the young Trudeau PMO staff. Tom Axworthy, who served as Trudeau's principal secretary from 1981 to 1984, recalls being told by Turner that he did not want his department bothered by "the junior G-men of the PMO."[12] Axworthy recently mused that "if he felt the Trudeau PMO was becoming too intrusive and that we were over-stepping our bounds, we can only imagine what he thinks of the Harper Government, where every ministerial communication must be vetted centrally, civil servants are kept on the shortest of leashes, and ministers are not even allowed to answer questions about their own departments in Question Period."[13]

Denis Smith, commenting in the Trudeau era, also warned, "We seem to have created in Canada a presidential system without its congressional advantages."[14]

Globe and Mail columnist Jeffrey Simpson has written of the increasing powers of the prime minister as a "friendly dictatorship": "The prime minister is the Sun King around whom all revolves and to whom all must pay homage."[15]

Those words were written in 2001 in reference to the Chrétien era. But, as Tom Axworthy notes, the Harper regime has taken prime ministerial powers to dangerous new heights, and there is no precedent for the vice grip on all aspects of the federal government currently being exercised by Prime Minister Stephen Harper. His government leaves virtually no role for his Cabinet members, much less for individual members of Parliament or for the House itself. As Don Martin wrote in the *National Post,* describing their behaviour during a recent government announcement, Harper's ministers "play the role usually reserved for potted palms."[16]

It is clear that Stephen Harper makes all the decisions in his government. With the possible exception of Minister of Finance Jim Flaherty, it does not appear that any of his ministers play a critical role even within their own portfolio areas. When the Harper government violated the contractual Atlantic Accord in the spring 2007 budget, the lead Atlantic Canada minister, Peter MacKay, had not been consulted. Like ordinary Canadians, he found out when the budget was tabled. Former minister of environment Rona Ambrose suggested that she was open to meeting the commitments of the Kyoto Protocol, until she was brought up short by statements from Prime Minister Harper.[17] When the Harper government decided to put forward a law that described Quebecers as a "nation" Minister for Intergovernmental Affairs Michael Chong resigned because he had not been consulted. Chong, honourable to the nth degree, remained a loyal, and quiet, backbencher. This is clearly *not* a Cabinet government.

Not only are Cabinet ministers denied a meaningful

role in the direction of their own portfolios, they are not trusted within the political orbit either. Each minister is able to have a small group of people working directly for him or her as political staff. The team spirit and loyalty to the boss of a minister's staff are generally taken for granted, but in his first term Stephen Harper's director of communications, Sandra Buckler, instructed the communications officers working on the ministers' personal staffs to report directly to her about whether their boss was doing a good job dealing with media.[18] Prior to this decision, the minister's team reported only to the minister. The level of distrust implicit in Harper's approach was shocking and unprecedented, but invisible to most Canadians.

Exercising control over every word a minister says is also new.[19] Under Prime Minister Harper, Cabinet members must submit speeches to the PMO for advance approval. As someone who frequently worked on speeches for my boss, Tom McMillan, there was never a time when speeches needed prior approval of the PMO. I recall Cabinet members in Paul Martin's government giving speeches without a note in front of them. (The brilliant John Godfrey and Stephen Owen are the only Canadian politicians I have ever seen perform this feat. Doing so allows the speaker to constantly seek eye contact, to stay focused on his or her listeners, to actually reach the audience. When politicians give a speech extemporaneously, they establish themselves as persons with real depth and knowledge.) Impromptu speechmaking is expressly forbidden in the Harper government. All speeches must be preapproved.

When newly appointed Environment Minister Rona Ambrose was to speak at the huge Biennial Globe Conference in Vancouver in 2006, her speech was nearly cancelled. An hour before her address, the PMO insisted that all references to "sustainable development" be removed. This was a challenging last-minute edict, as the conference topic is always "sustainable development."[20] A number of times, speeches expected from Minister Ambrose were abruptly cancelled.

Newfoundland Conservative MPs elected in 2006 figured out how to bypass PMO control over approval of all press releases. Since they could not get approvals in a timely way, they started calling the social pages editor of their local papers to get coverage of their activities.[21]

The control over ministers extends beyond their formal speeches. In many cases, Cabinet ministers are barred from responding to media inquiries. For example, following the 2007 Speech from the Throne, the PMO made it clear that the only ministers allowed to speak to the media would be Lawrence Cannon and Jim Prentice. Controlling the message is now the ultimate goal.

Given this priority, it is no wonder that Prime Minister Harper has also attempted to control the media. Early in his first term, PMO staff ordered the Parliamentary Press Gallery to provide lists of reporters who would ask questions and to hold reporters to an order of speaking. The press gallery responded by having the chosen PMO reporters walk away, leaving CBC-TV's Julie Van Dusen – known as a direct and effective journalist and, therefore, not on the PMO list of favoured reporters – as the first questioner. So Prime Minister Harper walked away.

Since 1965, the National Press Gallery has maintained a press theatre for the use of the government and the opposition alike. The press theatre is able to provide simultaneous translation, with cameras and wiring for broadcast quality in place. The press conferences are always chaired by a member of the Parliamentary Press Gallery. Unhappy with this situation, the Harper PMO developed a plan to create a facility much closer to that enjoyed by the U.S. president. The White House Press Theater is owned by the president. The facility is not used by anyone other than the president or his designate. The Harper PMO wanted the same arrangement.

In October 2007, the *Toronto Star* obtained evidence from Access to Information of the PMO's plans to convert a vacant shoe shop into a PMO press facility.[22] The vacant shoe store was in the Sparks Street Mall, a few steps from PMO headquarters at Langevin Block. The conversion from retail space to imperial media centre was described in the internal documents as a "special project for the PM, otherwise reffered [sic] as the Shoe Store Project." One document described the project as a "dedicated press availability facility," part of efforts to "put in place robust physical and information security measures to protect the Prime Minister and Cabinet."

It was about a lot more than security. The notes suggested there would be an advantage in being able to control the cameras and angles and give networks access only to PMO-approved camera angles. It was slated to cost $2 million, but it was hardly a passing fancy. When uncovered by the media, the Shoe Store Project had been in the works for over a year. Once revealed by the media it was trying to control, the project was dropped.

The same sort of desire may have done in the proposed National Portrait Gallery in Ottawa. The former U.S. Embassy is a beautiful old building, immediately across the street from Parliament Hill. Under Jean Chrétien, the building was slated to house the new gallery. The Harper PMO had other ideas. The PMO had visions of a grand ceremonial reception hall where Harper could greet visiting foreign dignitaries, with private meeting rooms and catering facilities.[23] The Harper government shifted the discussion of the gallery to a competition among other Canadian cities. Then, following the 2008 election, James Moore, the new minister for Canadian heritage, announced that there was no need for a National Portrait Gallery at all.

It stands to reason that a government so obsessed with control and "staying on message" would have insecurities about the vast, non-partisan civil service. The evolution of our civil service is beyond the scope of this book, but it plays a critical role in our democracy. In our earliest days, the civil service was anything but dispassionate. Sir John A. Macdonald placed his loyalists in key roles, and he was not the last prime minister to load the bureaucracy with those who served partisan interests. It was a long process to develop a civil service that was the envy of the world, but we did. For decades, our elected officials were advised by Ottawa mandarins for whom professionalism and dispassionate provision of expert policy advice were an art form. We need to restore the civil service to what it was at its best: a well-briefed, non-partisan group of professionals who have a depth of understanding of their areas of responsibility and a commitment to public service. Today's world and issues are so complex that we need this more than ever. Sadly, just as our need for such a civil service is critical, it is under assault.

The bureaucracy is now largely treated with contempt – with the exception of the increasingly powerful Clerk of the Privy Council. It was clear in the 2006 election that Stephen Harper viewed the bureaucracy as a partisan opposition. In the dying days of that campaign, as polls suggested he might win a majority, Harper sent an odd form of reassurance to those who feared what he might do with a majority. Essentially, he said that the critics need not worry because his efforts would be held in check by a civil service and a judiciary appointed by Liberals.

High-level appointees are treated as partisans and junior employees are treated as enemies. The evidence is everywhere. When a civil servant in the Canadian Food Inspection Agency shared his concerns about reduced inspection for food safety with his union, he was fired.

When Stephen Harper was angered by the interpretation of the *Elections Act* by Marc Mayrand, the head of Elections Canada, who said that veiled women would only have to show their faces at polling stations in private and with female officials, he attacked Elections Canada. "I have to say that it concerns me greatly, because the role of Elections Canada is not to make its own laws, it's to put into place the laws that Parliament has passed," Harper charged.[24] But others believed that Mayrand's ruling fairly interpreted the law. In order to force the interpretation the prime minister wanted and enforce visual identification of voters, the law was changed. And when Elections Canada refused to accept the financial reports from over fifty campaigns by Conservative candidates in the 2006 election due to overspending on advertising (the "In-Out Scandal"), the Harper Conservatives sued them.

The most egregious case of mistreatment of a senior civil servant was the firing of the president of the Canadian Nuclear Safety Commission (CNSC), Linda Keen. Keen is an internationally respected nuclear safety expert. She not only served as president of Canada's nuclear safety agency, she worked on nuclear safety standards for the International

Atomic Energy Agency. It was with real concern that she noted that the safety of some of Canada's oldest reactors was falling far behind global standards. The operations in Chalk River were particularly worrying. Its NRU reactor is a half-century old; it could never be licensed if built today. The reactor does not produce electricity. Rather it is an important global supplier of medical radioisotopes. In order to allow it to operate, the CNSC attached a condition to its relicensing. It required the owner, Crown corporation Atomic Energy of Canada Ltd., to install an additional electricity backup system sufficient to withstand damage from an earthquake.

The situation became critical in the fall of 2007. On November 18, 2007, AECL shut down the NRU reactor for routine maintenance. While it was closed, the regulator inspected and noticed the backup safety system had never been installed. The reactor was operating in violation of its licence. When the CNSC did what it must do under the law, insist that the reactor meet the conditions of its permit before restarting, AECL relied on its value in the medical isotope market and decided to defy the regulator.

Minister of Natural Resources Gary Lunn did not provide Minister of Health Tony Clement with any advance notice of the situation.[25] MDS Nordion, a commercial distributor of medical isotopes from NRU, itself once part of AECL before being spun off as a profit-making private sector operation, did not want to warn its competitors.

Other suppliers in the Netherlands and South Africa and France were not given the necessary heads-up to be able to increase production to meet an inevitable shortfall with the NRU reactor out of commission.

The stage was set for a preventable shortfall of diagnostic radionuclides. It was treated as an international crisis in the supply of "life-saving" radionuclides. In fact, the Nordion products were not for treatment, but for diagnosis. Still, it is essential to be diagnosed as quickly as possible and patients were up in arms.

In the House of Commons, the prime minister wasted no time in making it clear whom he held responsible. Certainly he did not hold his minister of natural resources responsible, nor the reactor operator. In Question Period, Harper took aim at the regulator. Rather than attack the whole of the CNSC, he attacked Linda Keen personally. Harper and Lunn argued that she should have taken into account the need for radionuclides in the global market even though it was clear that the legislation under which the CNSC operated would not have allowed such a consideration. How can a safety regulator be mandated for safety as well as for production targets? It has never been done in any field and for good reason: it would entrench an impossible conflict of interest. But the Harper government put forward amendments to mandate CNSC in the future to be concerned with the provision of radionuclides and not solely concerned with nuclear safety.

Within weeks, Keen had been fired from her post as president of the CNSC. Auditor General Sheila Fraser warned that the treatment of Linda Keen could have a chilling effect throughout the civil service.[26]

Our British style of parliamentary democracy evolved, first by reining in the power of the king and then by raising up the power of the people. Worryingly, in modern times, the power of the citizenry has been reduced by decreasing our impact on elected officials and on their scope for freedom of action. The pressures of increased technology, complex policy questions, a world war, the television era have all led to more power being placed in the hands of fewer and fewer people. In Canada, as in other modern democracies, the last fifty years have seen an increasing centralization of power, first shifting from Parliament to Cabinet, and then from Cabinet to the prime minister. We risk losing the democratic progress of centuries in wresting power from a king only to see it vested in an increasingly unaccountable and autocratic prime minister.

If under Stephen Harper the level of control from PMO has become more extreme, does that really affect the workings of government? Is democracy really compromised by a "friendly dictatorship"? The following chapters explore this important question.

Chapter 2

Parliament as Anachronism?

In the Westminster tradition, Parliament – the whole assembly of members of Parliament meeting in the House of Commons, with the largely symbolic but useful Senate as a chamber of "sober, second thought," – *is* the government. The prime minister is first among equals. The leader of the official opposition is also part of the government. In fact, the full title is "Her Majesty's Loyal Opposition," because all members of Parliament are loyal to the head of state: the queen as represented by the governor general.

The process of ever-increasing centralization of power has changed the nature of Parliament. It is hard now to identify areas where individual members of Parliament have any real power at all. This is especially the case when they serve within a political party that enforces discipline on votes and controls access to the media. Individual members of Parliament can have enormous power when they are sitting as Independents in a minority parliament. The most powerful example of such influence, in recent years, is that of the late Chuck Cadman, who voted with the Liberals on a budget motion on May 19, 2005, thereby allowing Paul Martin's government to remain in power. The power of that example is fortified by its rarity. Increasingly individual members of Parliament have very little scope for real action at all. Backbenchers used to look to the possibility of promotion to Cabinet where the real power lay, but even there power has been centralized. Cabinet ministers are less and less in control of their own portfolios.

To keep absolute control on so many aspects of governmental actions and communications does take more than Stephen Harper alone. It takes a machine. And the machinery of government is driven increasingly by one other man – the Clerk of the Privy Council Office (PCO).

Prime Minister Harper has done away with the role of a highly visible second-in-command in the form of a deputy prime minister. Prime Minister Trudeau had created the role and every prime minister since has followed suit. Mulroney had Don Mazankowski; Chrétien had first Sheila Copps and then Herb Grey. Paul Martin elevated Anne McLellan to the role. Stephen Harper signalled how totally he was to be in control by abandoning the position altogether. Since Trudeau, the deputy PM has worked closely with PCO, providing the political interface between the most powerful arm of the civil service and the political whirlwind that is the Prime Minister's Office.

Under Harper, the Clerk of the Privy Council Office works extremely closely with the PM. *Globe and Mail* columnist Lawrence Martin has argued that the Clerk is the second most powerful man in Ottawa, essentially the deputy prime minister. The Clerk is secretary to the prime minister, secretary to the Cabinet, and head of the entire public service. Martin quotes a senior official as saying, "No one outside this place has any idea who the hell he is."[1]

Cape Bretoners know Kevin Lynch as the son of kindly Dr. Lynch, the doctor employed by the Sydney steel mill where workers died from pollution-related illnesses around the time they got their pension. Ottawa insiders know that Kevin Lynch is a highly intelligent, shrewd and exacting economist. He had risen through the ranks at Finance Canada when Stephen Harper chose him as Clerk of the Privy Council.

Patrice Dutil, political scientist at Ryerson University and author of *Searching for Leadership,* a study on secretaries to Cabinet, has said, "It's government by thunderbolt. The PM decides what he wants to do and he does it not through his cabinet but through his clerk."[2]

Donald Savoie, a University of Moncton professor well known for documenting the increasing centralization of power in government, agrees with Dutil that the Harper government has increased the power of the Clerk. Savoie has outlined how the Canadian prime minister has more power than the American president or the British prime minister. While the powers of a Canadian prime minister obviously exceed those of an American president who faces a separate legislative and judicial branch, his or her advantages over the resident of Number 10 Downing Street are not immediately apparent. As Savoie points out, the British system cleaves more closely to the notion that the prime minister is first among equals. As such, the government party's caucus can remove its leader. In Canada, the major parties can only remove their leader in a convention of the membership. So too does the Canadian Clerk have more power than his American or British counterparts.

Just as the growth in the prime minister's powers began under Pierre Trudeau, so did the growth in the role of the Clerk. Michael Pitfield was Clerk to Trudeau and shifted the role from civil service support to Cabinet to support for the prime minister and his office. This role became formalized in the early 1990s. Many believe that the increased centralization of powers was in response to the new *Access to Information Act* (1985). I can recall being asked by the deputy minister of environment not to write as many helpful notes, as they might end up being accessed. As Lawrence Martin observes, "Prime Ministers saw potential land mines everywhere and moved to exert far greater controls over information flows, sending a chill through the system that has increased with time."[3]

Evidence that PCO is better at denying access than allowing it – a freedom *from* information system – is abundant. Information Commissioner Robert Marleau gave the PCO a grade of F in 2007 for obstructing access and for contributing to less and less transparency in the operations of government.[4] (Clearly some sensitive information is legitimately withheld for its impact on national security or for confidentiality considerations. Such documents can be legitimately expurgated. Nevertheless, access to information requests should be answered promptly. Sunshine is a great antiseptic.)

With the extraordinary massing of power within PCO and especially in the person of Kevin Lynch, people are increasingly asking whether there is a blurring of the Clerk's role into the explicitly political. For example, Lynch played a key role in the highly political mess surrounding the leak of a diplomatic cable detailing a meeting between a member of Barack Obama's team and the Canadian mission in Chicago. When it appeared that someone in the Harper government had leaked to the media the memo documenting an Obama advisor reassuring Canada that Obama's position favouring renegotiation of NAFTA was merely election posturing, it was Lynch who was asked to oversee the investigation. The choice was surprising. Usually such a review of leaks of sensitive and confidential federal information would be undertaken by the RCMP.

Lynch took over and chose to outsource the investigation to an American private sector security firm. Journalists were not particularly surprised when the report white-washed the involvement of PMO staff, choosing instead to blame an anonymous foreign affairs bureaucrat. The report's conclusions were circumstantial, alleging that so many people had been emailed the diplomatic report, including to non-secure email addresses, that it was impossible to iden-tify who was responsible. As *the Toronto Star*'s James Travers noted, Lynch had "spent three months and some $140,000 only to scratch his head. 'The investigation has been unable to determine who leaked the report, to whom it was leaked or whether there was only one leak.'"[5]

Of course, exculpating the PMO political hacks was not without cost to our international reputation. The whole incident was a black eye to Canadian foreign relations. What foreign governmental representative will want to share anything with Canadian embassies around the world if our routine email system is so leaky that confidential material ends up on CNN?

The problem is that the "official story" just didn't add up. As Travers points out, it was the work of a moment to connect the dots between people in Harper's office and prominent U.S. Republicans:

> Multiple sources say the Canadian note questioning the Democrat frontrunner's public promise to reopen NAFTA was leaked from the Prime Minister's Office to

a Republican contact before it made American head-
line news.

Their claims come days after an internal probe
threw up its hands at finding the source. Contradicting
Friday's inconclusive report, they claim the controversial memo was slipped to the son of Wisconsin
Republican Congressman James Sensenbrenner. Frank
Sensenbrenner is well connected to Harper's inner
circle and, at Ottawa's insistence, was briefly on contract with Canada's Washington embassy to work on
congressional relations.[6]

But the Clerk-led investigation never looked in that direction.

That leak was way out of bounds in terms of interference in the domestic affairs of another nation. Known
in the United States as "NAFTA-gate," the media uproar
was credited with losing Obama the Ohio primary, even
though the first leak from the prime minister's then-chief
of staff Ian Brodie attempted to smear Hillary Clinton.

Another political football handled by PCO was the
arrest of alleged terrorists. The *Globe and Mail* reported in
September 2007 about the PCO's control over communications in the case of eighteen Toronto-area young Islamic
men. Reporter Omar El Akkad received over 1,700 pages
of documents in response to an access to information
request. One PCO memo read: "Just so we're all clear . . .

in particular on issues of this nature with many depts involved ALL electronic media interviews must be co-ordinated and OK'd by pco [sic]."[7]

Although usually vetted by the PMO, Minister for Public Safety Stockwell Day's talking points regarding the case had to be approved by the PCO. Consistent with the tight controls on Conservative Cabinet ministers, Day was not permitted to speak off the cuff. What made this unusual was that the non-political civil service hub was in charge of his talking points.

The culture of the Harper government is "take no prisoners" partisanship. The gradual Americanization of our political life is typified by a state of constant electioneering. All levers of government have shifted from governance to electoral advantage. It was certainly always the case that governments made decisions with an eye to gaining public support and votes in the next election, but the Harper government's approach has taken it from a factor to the primary operating directive of the entirety of government. Tom Axworthy, former principal secretary to Pierre Trudeau, has described the current situation as "constant attack ads, 24 hour permanent campaigning and the dumbing down of political discourse."[8]

Whereas in the parliamentary tradition, it was common to experience non-partisan cooperation in the House of Commons, the current Parliament is typified by un-relenting partisanship. Whereas the House of Commons committees once typically worked in a cooperative fashion, the PMO has pressed its committee chairs to obstruct progress and restrict unfriendly witnesses.

Cooperation was once so accepted that one of the most respected texts on Canadian government, by two of Canada's outstanding political scientists, R. MacGregor Dawson and his son W. F. Dawson, asserted its role in uncontroversial terms. *The Government of Canada* was first written in 1949, with subsequent updates and a new version, revised by Norman Ward, in 1989. The current version available for students of political science explains:

> It must not be supposed that the members of the government and the opposition parties conduct the business of Parliament in an atmosphere of hate and distrust. The personnel of individual Parliaments varies, of course, and televised question periods may convey the impression that the last sentence is untrue. But question period has become a public performance; proceedings generally are rarely bitter, and the parties generally consult and co-operate amicably with one another in making many informal arrangements for the benefit of all. . . . A spirit of compromise and fairness usually prevails; and the parliamentary struggle sometimes seems to be a game among contestants who derive a common advantage from seeing that the general amenities are preserved.[9]

Given the toxic atmosphere of Parliament today, the text is in need of further revision.

Memories of a more cooperative style of government are not completely lost. Former prime minister John Turner recently recalled his approach to the passage of legislation when he was minister of justice under Pierre Trudeau. When he wanted to bring in a legislative reform, he would start by inviting the justice critics from the opposition parties to a dinner. Over a meal and wine, he would put forward informally what he had in mind. This started a process to build consensus about a new law before it ever received first reading. "By the time I put the bill forward, it was as good as passed because the opposition was on board," recalled Turner in 2008.[10]

My own experience in government was quite similar. Serving from 1986 to 1988 as senior policy advisor to Tom McMillan, the federal minister of environment in the Mulroney government, I was frequently directed to keep the opposition critics up to speed on key files. From acid rain to negotiations to protect the ozone layer, opposition critics were kept informed. So too were the provincial ministers of the environment. I had not realized at the time what a glorious era it was for cooperation. Ontario Environment Minister Jim Bradley and Quebec Environment Minister Clifford Lincoln are among Canada's most dedicated environmentalists. They both held provincial environmental reins for the Liberals, battling it out with a Progressive

Conservative government in Ottawa. Meanwhile the federal minister of environment also wanted a record as the nation's greenest minister. This mood of healthy competition to do more for the environment was both unprecedented and, as yet, has never been duplicated.

As a result, the seven eastern provinces agreed to binding reductions of acid rain. The eastern provinces, responsible for the most sulphur dioxide, agreed to 50 percent reductions. Once Canada had established its bone fides, the federal government approached the U.S. government of Ronald Reagan with clean hands. For the first time, an environmental issue enjoyed the position of top priority in bilateral relations with the most powerful nation on earth. Stan Darling, backbench Progressive Conservative MP for Parry Sound–Muskoka, had long been a champion for real action, as had former environment minister under Joe Clark, John Fraser; Liberal MP Charles Caccia; and Liberal Leader John Turner.

The most inspiring example of cooperation was the effort to protect the southern third of the Haida Gwaii/ Queen Charlotte Islands archipelago, known as South Moresby. When I joined the minister's staff in the summer of 1986, Tom McMillan had already pledged to make South Moresby a national park.[11]

Tom McMillan's commitment to save South Moresby was made without prior Cabinet approval or PMO oversight. It came during the 1985 Parks Congress in Banff, celebrating one hundred years of the national park system. Moments before stepping up to the podium, Tom McMillan penned in changes to his speech. There was a large cake on display for the minister to cut in celebration of the Parks Centenary. McMillan waved away the cake saying it should not be cut until South Moresby was protected as a national park – earning an exuberant standing ovation for the most significant wilderness conservation pledge in living memory.[12]

The ancient temperate rainforests of the area contained trees as old as 2,000 years, with a variety of species, some unique in the world. Escaping ice cover in the last Ice Age, the region became a refugium for species that otherwise would have been extinct. For that reason it was dubbed "Canada's Galapagos."

There had been Haida Nation blockades on the logging roads and special features on David Suzuki's *The Nature of Things* television program. "Saving South Moresby" was the premier environmental issue for the country. Environment Canada was getting more letters about South Moresby than on acid rain – a point Tom McMillan made to his boss, Brian Mulroney, when pitching why the PM should become involved when negotiations became stalled. The ultra-conservative Socred government of B.C. Premier William Vander Zalm was strongly in favour of logging the ancient trees. As forest fibre each tree could be valued as high as $20,000.

The most environmentally diligent of parliamentarians, Charles Caccia, who was environment minister under Trudeau, had long championed protection of South Moresby. As luck would have it, the MP for the area, Jim Fulton, was also the NDP environment critic and strongly in favour of protection. The Speaker of the House at the time, John Fraser, was from B.C. too, and a lifelong conservationist. (Fraser was also Canada's first elected Speaker.)

Ironically, the biggest federal political opposition to protecting South Moresby came from the ranks of the minister's own party. Some of the Progressive Conservative caucus elected from British Columbia — MPs like Lorne McCuish, Benno Friesen, Gerry St. Germain, Fred King, and Lorne Greenaway — wanted to help their provincial cousins, the far-right Socred Party, do the industry's bidding. Tom McMillan, a Red Tory (a long-lost breed of socially progressive Conservative) also from P.E.I., used to joke that some of the B.C. caucus thought he was a communist. Working across party lines was essential.

Cross-party cooperation reached its zenith when Jim Fulton tabled an Opposition Day motion calling for the protection of South Moresby. An Opposition Day motion mandates that the government party and all opposition parties dedicate House time to a debate on the issue selected by the opposition. The motion is not put to a vote. Opposition Days are usually dreaded by the minister whose portfolio is targeted. On one day's notice, speeches have to be prepared and other MPs found to speak in favour of the government's position. Meanwhile, it is a platform for the opposition to berate the government all day long.

The day Jim Fulton's motion came through, there was jubilation in McMillan's office. I started drafting speeches for the other government representatives and called Jim Fulton to thank him.

As the debate unfolded, the president of the Council of the Haida Nation, Miles Richardson, was watching the live coverage on CPAC from Haida Gwaii. It was a rare day of total unanimity from all sides of the House. Or at least it looked like that on television. In the government lobby, just out of sight, some of the B.C. Conservative MPs who wanted to see more chainsaws in the forest were trying to convince other Conservatives they should refuse to speak in favour of the motion. Meanwhile, Vince Dantzer, Conservative MP from Okanagan, who argued for preservation, quipped: "This is more like a love-in than a debate."[13]

On the floor of the House, Bill Blaikie, MP from Winnipeg, a former United Church minister and also former NDP environment critic, seized the moment and suggested that the motion should be deemed to be passed unanimously. Tom McMillan agreed immediately, calling it "an inspired suggestion." The Liberals were represented by Brian Tobin, a Newfoundland Liberal MP. Tobin, speaking on behalf of John Turner, leader of the official opposition, was quick to agree.

Speaker of the House John Fraser chose his words carefully. Parliamentary alchemy – the conversion of a non-votable motion during debate to be deemed to have passed unanimously at the end of the debate – requires caution. The House was master of its own process. While there was no precedent for a non-votable opposition motion being deemed to have passed unanimously, Fraser ruled that with the will of the House anything was possible. The Speaker gave a deliberate pause, like an auctioneer . . . waiting not for a higher bid, but for an objection. Three times he asked, "Honourable Members have heard the motion. Is it agreed?" Fortunately, the pro-logging MPs were still in the government lobby twisting arms.

When the Speaker ruled that the motion to declare South Moresby a national park was deemed to have been passed unanimously, Miles Richardson said, "Today the Great Spirit hovered over the House of Commons." John Fraser referred to the South Moresby campaign as being part of "the conspiracy to save the planet."

Such cooperation is so unusual in today's context that distortions of this story have led to media articles alleging I violated my boss's trust by talking to the opposition.[14]

There was another great moment in pan-partisan cooperation in that year. In the summer of 1987, Prime Minister Mulroney called for a free vote in the House on the issue of capital punishment. Despite my abiding love for democracy and MP empowerment, it was frightening to contemplate a free vote that might lead to Canada moving backwards and accepting state-sanctioned murder. I watched the vote from the gallery of the House with tension in the air as each MP stood to register his or her choice. When the Clerk read out the *yeas* and *nays,* confirming that Canada would remain a non-capital punishment society, the cheers erupted from all sides of the House. The then minister for the status of women and future foreign affairs minister, Barbara McDougall, face alight in joy, raced across the aisle to embrace NDP MP Nelson Riis. It was clear in that moment that the two had been working the phones, collaborating in their shared, non-partisan commitment to ensure that Canada would not retreat from opposition to killing its citizens. The genuine sharing of a principled commitment transcended partisanship.

While full cooperation in the House was not routine, it was hardly unusual and had its greatest expression in the work of parliamentary committees. While Tom McMillan did not take the John Turner approach of building consensus before his bills were drafted, he did have a willingness to accept opposition amendments in the House. The House Environment Committee, then chaired by former minister in the Clark government and ex-ambassador to Ethiopia David MacDonald, spent considerable time on the controversial *Canadian Environmental Protection Act*. The act was an attempt to provide comprehensive regulation of toxic chemicals, from cradle to grave. It had a number of serious gaps. Due to internal jurisdictional turf wars, it did not cover pesticides or radionuclides. But it did combine the existing laws on commercial chemicals, ocean dumping, and a number of other housekeeping matters. It offered the hope of being able to track and control toxic substances from the laboratory to commercial use to disposal, but it did so one chemical at a time. One now well-accepted centrepiece of the act, the Priority Substances List, was not included at first reading. A brilliant environmental activist, Kai Millyard, was working for Friends of the Earth (FOE) at the time and attended every committee hearing. The environmental community worried that the bill's approach of dealing with one substance at a time would make it impossible to deal with the backlog of dangerous substances. FOE and other groups, including the minister's own advisory council, came up with the idea of a way to kick-start the listing with a Priority Substances List. A Progressive Conservative backbencher on the committee, Bob Wenman, agreed to put forward some of FOE's amendments. They passed and, contrary to many amendments passed in committee in recent years, the government accepted them.

Over the last twenty years, the shrinking scope for effective action by MPs has attracted attention. Former prime minister Paul Martin spoke out about it, coining the term "democratic deficit." While he awaited the moment when he could replace his nemesis, Jean Chrétien, he spoke frequently of the need to rebalance the role of MPs with that of Cabinet-style government. Most of this deficit was located in the operations of the House. Martin promised to make changes to increase the role of the individual MP, backbencher or opposition member, who felt that the great work of the government of Canada passed them by.[15]As elected members, they objected to being treated like part of the furniture.

The control of committees was one of the areas identified by Paul Martin as being in need of reform. In relation to the workings of committees, Martin changed the rules so that committee members could elect their own chair. He promised more free votes in the House and more independence for the individual member.

The election of chairs did seem like a positive step, although many MPs did not feel that the democratic deficit had yet been addressed. MPs often feel entirely powerless. One of my most unusual opportunities to meet with MPs on a completely informal basis was when I went on a hunger strike on Parliament Hill. In May 2000, I decided that the plight of Sydney, Nova Scotia, families living with toxic waste in their backyards and basements would never be addressed without a constant reminder on Parliament Hill. My "post" was immediately opposite the members' entrance on the west side of Centre Block. Over the seventeen days I was there I became part of the furniture, and chatting with me was a safe zone for members wanting to vent their frustrations. I sometimes joked that I should have a kiosk like Lucy in the *Peanuts* comic with a sign reading "The psychiatrist is IN." MPs would come out and stand next to me while I sat on a lawn chair across from the main entrance to the House lobby. The comments were generally the same, regardless of whether they came from members of government or of the opposition parties: "I honestly don't know what I am doing here. I mean I cannot get anything done . . . If we could concentrate on anything for more than fifteen minutes maybe we could do something . . . I have my committee work and then the leader asks me to take on another project . . . I wish I was home on the farm where I felt like I accomplished something."

The role of the individual MP has been sidelined by the power of Cabinet, and now by the PM alone.

I have been attending hearings of parliamentary committees for nearly thirty years, and I have never seen anything like the obstruction and political sabotage that have occurred since the 2006 election. At one point in 2008 over six committees were in gridlock due to filibusters.

In Canada, parliamentary filibustering is relatively rare. A true filibuster occurs when a member of a legislature, once given the floor, refuses to yield it. In the British parliamentary tradition, it used to be called "talking out." As long as the elected member can stand and continue to speak – without a break – the work of that legislative body is arrested. The longest one-man filibuster in the House of Commons was that of Bob Mills, Alliance MP from Red

Deer, Alberta. Stephen Harper was then the leader of the Alliance Party and it was the only party to deny the scientific case on global warming. In 2002, the party objected to the Kyoto Protocol on the grounds that there was not enough scientific evidence that there even was a real threat due to climate change. The Progressive Conservatives also voted against Kyoto, but as leader Joe Clark explained at the time, only because he objected to Chrétien's approach. Clark felt Chrétien had unnecessarily alienated the provinces. The Progressive Conservative Party understood the science and wanted real action to reduce greenhouse gases. In contrast, the Alliance Party was sending out fundraising letters under Stephen Harper's signature alleging Kyoto was a "socialist scheme."[16]

Although Kyoto could easily have been ratified by an Order in Council, just as Mulroney used Orders in Council to ratify the two major treaties from the 1992 Rio Earth Summit – the UN Framework Convention on Climate Change and the Biodiversity Convention – Chrétien wanted a bit of theatre and opted for a ratification vote in the House of Commons.

Bob Mills was the Alliance Party environment critic and took to the floor in debate, refusing to keep to his time or yield – all in an effort to stop Canada playing a responsible role in international action to protect future generations.

As rare as filibusters have been in the House, they have never played a role in the workings of the committees until this past year. There have been a number of filibusters during the 2007–08 parliamentary session, including within the Environment Committee – chaired by Bob Mills. It must be said that despite his party's views on Kyoto, Mills was very dedicated to the greening of Canada. He was a supporter of a revolution to renewable energy. In his early years, through the 1970s, he had been part of the movement for a "conserver society," arguably the precursor of the call for sustainable development. If Stephen Harper had been looking for someone in his party who actually cared about the issue, he couldn't have found a better minister than Mills. Sadly, he was bypassed for Cabinet.

In a breach with the steps undertaken by Martin to address the democratic deficit through allowing committee members to elect committee chairs, Harper decided to appoint them once again. The charade of a vote remained, but committee members could only choose among the names put forward by the PMO. This is how Mills became chair of the Environment Committee.

The legislation coming through the Environment Committee was predominantly related to air quality and climate. The first bill was drafted by the government. Called the *Clean Air Act,* it operated to treat air pollutants as the priority while actually disallowing action on climate. Through the work in the committee, where, due to the government's minority status the opposition members had the power to pass amendments, the bill was completely rewritten. What emerged would have been excellent legislation. The Harper government never brought it forth for third reading.

Since then the committee has dealt with a number of other climate-related bills. The private member's bill put forward by Liberal Pablo Rodriguez, the *Kyoto Implementation Act,* actually passed on February 14, 2007. Despite statements by the prime minister that he would respect any bill passed by the House, this law has been completely ignored.

The Harper government must have realized that it was not winning any points in the court of public opinion by ignoring laws passed by Parliament. A new tactic was needed. The Conservatives needed to kill good bills *before* they could become law and filibusters came to committee.

As a climate bill put forward by NDP leader Jack Layton, Bill 377, made its way to the Environment Committee, government members began to obstruct the deliberations. On any procedural motion, they would start talking and not stop. The work of the committee ground to a halt for months. Speakers were not required to stand and speak non-stop for months. They were seated and could obtain breaks as needed. The committee hearings rarely went beyond the time allotted, so a 3 P.M. to 5 P.M. filibuster would resume two days later, running again from 3 P.M. to 5 P.M. If they decided to meet late, the filibuster would pause long enough to order in dinner for the MPs. A typical time waster occurred when government members spoke for hours about the unfairness of the NDP motion to limit debate to two minutes per MP per clause.

In a flourish of moronic bravado, Jeff Watson, Conservative MP for Essex, pulled his McDonald's meal from his briefcase and plunked it next to his microphone. The gambit was Watson's way of saying, "I have my dinner so I can talk for hours, so go order some food." When asked how long his intervention might be, he grinned and shot back, "Stay tuned."

Hours later, when Watson finished, Mark Warawa, parliamentary secretary to then-Environment Minister John Baird and MP from Langley, B.C., took over. He spoke in lofty terms of free speech, linking his right to strangle climate change legislation to the anniversary of Vimy Ridge, as if Canadian lives were lost to protect his right to arrest democratic debate in the House committee. He invoked Lord Wilberforce and his valiant fight to abolish slavery in the British Empire, claiming that Wilberforce had spoken in the British Parliament for forty years to end slavery. "Not in one go," quipped Liberal MP John Godfrey.

It was clear that the master of filibuster himself, Bob Mills, was growing impatient with his colleagues. There was simply no way to move forward. On one occasion, he actually said, "I'd like everyone to shut up." And later that same day, "Maybe you could all go out behind the barn, but that's a place I don't want to go . . ."[17] After consulting with all members of the committee privately, he tried to put forward a motion to ask for advice and direction from the "Process and Procedures Committee, or some other appropriate body." NDP environment critic Nathan Cullen pointed out that the Process and Procedures Committee itself was one of the committees blocked by filibusters. Wearily, Mills replied, "Yes, that's why I added 'or some other appropriate body.'"

The House committees have descended into farce.

The obstruction of committees has not been restricted to filibusters. Government members of committees have been aggressive in blocking witnesses unfriendly to the government's views. When opposition members have succeeded in getting independent witnesses before the committee, their testimony has been halted by the chair.

In May 2007, the Commons Standing Committee on International Trade was examining the Security and Prosperity Partnership. An expert on its implications for energy policy, Gordon Laxer, from the Parkland Institute in Alberta, was beginning to explain his organization's concern. The SPP places a priority on "energy security," but as Laxer described how hard-wiring energy supply from Canada to the United States left the eastern provinces vulnerable because they depend on imports from overseas, he was cut off by Leon Benoit, Conservative chair of the committee. Benoit told Laxer his testimony was irrelevant and ordered him to stop testifying. The contretemps that ensued pitted the Conservative MPs against the opposition

MPs. A vote was demanded by the opposition MPs and the majority voted that the testimony was relevant and germane.

Then things took a turn to the truly bizarre. The chair threw down his pen, declared the meeting adjourned, and stormed from the room. The Conservative members of the committee left with him. The tactic — and it was a tactic — created a procedural quandary. There was no way to continue the hearing in the absence of the chair. The Liberal MPs stayed on with Laxer, but the hearing was in limbo. Laxer left without being able to complete his evidence.[18]

That was on May 10. On May 15, another committee disintegrated as the chair refused to allow the will of the members to set its agenda. The House Committee on Official Languages had voted to review the implications of the cancellation of the Court Challenges Program on minority language rights. The Conservative chair of the committee, Guy Lauzon, refused to allow the hearing to proceed, so opposition members voted to remove him as chair. The work of the committee ground to a halt as the government refused to appoint a new chair.[19]

While the small number of close observers of Parliament watched the increasingly dysfunctional House teeter on the edge of anarchy, an explanation for the antics came from the pages of the *National Post*. Don Martin, Ottawa political watcher for the *Post,* had been chatting with a Conservative chair of a committee. The conversation centred on the growing use of filibusters and the abrupt termination of meetings in defiance of all procedure. The fellow mentioned almost casually, "It's all in the handbook." Martin was incredulous: "You mean there's an actual handbook telling Conservative chairs how to do this?" Yes, indeed, there is.

The handbook is several hundred pages and Martin is the only journalist to have a copy, although he allowed me to have a peek. Entitled *In the Hot Seat: An Evening Primer for Committee Chairs,* it sets out how to ensure committee witnesses are favourable to the government's positions and how to strangle opposition motions in procedural red tape through long-winded rulings from the chair sprinkled with frequent references to respected works on parliamentary procedure. Sample speeches are ready-made for committee chairs. When looking through the handbook, I realized I had heard Bob Mills deliver portions of the canned speech entitled, "Defending a Ruling that a Motion to Put the Question Is Out of Order." It is nearly incomprehensible, but has the benefit of being extremely long, replete with reading into the record pages of rules of parliamentary practice from the book *House of Commons Procedure and Practice,* by Robert Marleau and Camille Montpetit.

Further advice for committee chairs includes the throwing-down-a-pencil-and-storming-out-of-the-room gambit. It even suggests all Conservative members should be prepared to walk out from time to time if the committee's work is not going the government's way. Here is one extract:

> Once vote called, either have CPC members vote
> against the matter or at least abstain from the vote.
> Alternatively, CPC members could consider refusing
> to deal with the matter and simply leave the room so
> as not be party to this charade. (Protect CPC party
> from broad the strokes of the media [sic].)

All of the ungrammatical, nonsensical aspects of that paragraph are as they appear in the handbook. Here is another typical bit of advice: "Eventually the opposition will wise up that they need to adjourn debate on the motion before they can vote on it."

The committee chair handbook is all part of the conversion of the House as government to the House as organ for communicating the political and partisan message of the Harper PMO. The chairs are constantly reminded to "avoid bad press, to limit opposition rhetoric, protect the interests of the party." As one bullet point puts it: "Consider the political 'Big Picture' and the role that committee plays within the Big Picture."

With the re-election of a Conservative minority in October 2008, the issue of the chair handbook, referred to as the "committee obstruction manual," was discussed by

Harper's new chief government whip, former defence minister Gordon O'Connor. He told *The Hill Times:*

> What it is in reality is it's like the *Cole's Notes* of what committee chairs should think about, or how to operate in committees . . . I think there's a need for that certainly for people who will be chairs from our side, but what I'm going to do is I'm going to go through the book – if you want to call it that, but it's just a bunch of sheets of paper – and I think I'll try to refine it and improve it so that it's focused on how to be an effective chair.[20]

His comments were made in the brief period, post-election, when the Harper government sought to send out signals that it intended to be more collaborative in the new Parliament. Such warm and fuzzy notions were blown away within days by the incendiary economic statement on November 27, 2008 and the parliamentary crisis that ensued. The attempt to use the economic crisis as cover for the most bare-knuckled attempt in Canadian political history to annihilate opposition parties led to their rapid coalescing in a planned non-confidence vote. The use of government levers of power for purely partisan advantage has never been as transparent.

The backdrop for all of this conflict has been the obvious rudeness and partisan bickering of Question

Period. Canadians tend to assume that Question Period has always been as bad as it is now. The truth is that in all areas of our culture expectations for civility have declined. Older people do not find younger ones springing up to offer a seat on a bus. Drivers cut others off, gunning the engine as they do so. Expressions of abuse, whether through obscene gestures or casual expletives, have become common. Nevertheless, one might wish that the seat of our government would operate in ways that raise the bar, rather than plumb the depths.

Historically, Question Period has provided moments of clever repartee and inspired oration. The work of the Speaker in keeping order was not always onerous. Poor behaviour would result in a loss of points and reduction of influence. The Speaker holds a number of powers to keep the House functioning. He can force a minister to make his or her answer responsive to the question, and discipline a member for repeating the same argument or for raising matters irrelevant to the question asked. He can discipline members who violate rules of decorum by refusing to recognize them in the House for as long as he feels is appropriate. And there is actually a Standing Order of Parliament, number 16, that requires members to be quiet and not interrupt another who is asking or answering a question. It also states that when the Speaker rises, all members are to sit down and be silent. No questions are ever to be asked directly across the floor, but are to be always directed through the Speaker. This formality is meant to preserve the notion of respect for the House and its members and, by extension, the people of Canada.

Question Period undoubtedly changed when television cameras were allowed in the chamber. Still, even after the advent of live broadcasts, the essence of Question Period's usefulness remained. In the Dawsons' classic text on Canadian government, Question Period was described as a good way to root out important information:

> The question must be simple and direct, and neither it nor the answer are debatable. The ability to question the government in this way is an invaluable privilege, for it enables the opposition to keep in close touch with the administration and to draw out many hidden matters into the light of day . . . A number of safeguards have been raised against the abuse of the interrogation; but, generally speaking, the minister will find it difficult to withhold any information which is requested unless he can plead that to give it would be contrary to the public interest.[21]

In my experience on a minister's staff, Question Period could descend to the raucous, but it happened rarely. There were still days when Canadian parliamentarians attempted to reach for Churchillian rhetoric, even if they fell short. Ministers' staffs anticipated questions and prepared a proper response. My former boss, Tom McMillan, used to try to be eloquent and informative in his responses. The occasional partisan barb was good for fun, but the question had to be addressed, if not fully answered. Quite often further response would be sent to opposition members in writing.

The late Jim Fulton, NDP environment critic, pushed the limits of proper behaviour in 1985 by smuggling a dead salmon into the House and crossing the floor to plunk it down on a startled Brian Mulroney's desk. He violated so many rules of the House that it was hard to add them all up. One cardinal rule is that no props are allowed, and a dead salmon was one serious prop. John Fraser and Jim Fulton, despite their political differences, were friends. When he was contemplating running for Speaker in 1986, Fraser told Fulton that if he had been in the role when Fulton pulled that stunt he would have refused to recognize him in the House for six months. As it was, Fulton was disciplined for a lesser stretch of silence.

The member who felt most aggrieved by the salmon incident was neither Fraser nor Mulroney, but another NDP member and Fulton's benchmate, Margaret Mitchell. Mitchell was in her sixties and always appeared a proper lady in the House. As time came for Fulton's moment on the roster for Question Period, she was horrified as, seated and out of sight to all but his benchmate, he began to undo his belt buckle. When he began to loosen his trousers, she became alarmed, and as he proceeded to draw up from his trouser leg something large and black she nearly fainted. It is, of course, challenging to smuggle an adult dead Pacific salmon into the House, and Jim had ingeniously secreted it down the leg of his trousers in a garbage bag.[22]

There are other memorable moments of rules broken in the House. Progressive Conservative minister John Crosbie's famous barb at Sheila Copps, claiming she put him in mind of the song lyrics "Pass the Tequila, Sheila, lie down and love me tonight," may seem tame in comparison with today's daily outrages, but was then seen as unparliamentary in the extreme. Usually, Crosbie's love of colourful language stayed within parliamentary bounds and he was a good parliamentarian.

The question of which factor has been more corrosive to House civility – the advent of television or the fact that since 1984 the Speaker has been elected – could occupy academics for decades, but the trend has been for consecutive Speakers to be increasingly unwilling to enforce the rules. Decorum in the House requires that the Speaker enforce the rules and that the government in power and opposition members respect them. This is where things have most deteriorated.

Every question delivered to the current prime minister by the Speaker is treated as an excuse to attack the questioner. One chilling example is the series of replies to questions about the treatment of men taken prisoner by Canadian soldiers and turned over to the Afghanistan government as suspected Taliban members. When Leader of the Official Opposition Stéphane Dion asked for information about whether press reports of ill treatment were accurate, Stephen Harper attacked Dion and questioned why he cared more about the Taliban than our own soldiers. On March 21, 2007, I actually felt the air being squashed from my lungs, so deep was my shock at this answer from the prime minister: "I can understand the passion that the Leader of the Opposition and members of his party feel for Taliban prisoners. I just wish occasionally they would show the same passion for Canadian soldiers."[23]

Then Foreign Affairs Minister Peter MacKay used the same tactic. Any question about whether Canada was respecting the Geneva Convention was used as a club to beat opposition members by alleging that even asking the question suggested Taliban sympathies. Once, the prime minister used a question from the Liberal leader about the treatment of Afghan prisoners as an excuse to attack me.[24] Sitting in the gallery in the House is painful enough without being the object of the prime minister's disgraceful attempt to avoid answering the question by attacking elsewhere.

Another approach in Question Period is Conservative ministers' constant use of quotes from third parties, often out of context, to defend government policies. Environment minister John Baird used quotes from former U.S. vice president Al Gore to suggest Gore applauded Harper's approach to the climate crisis, until Gore had to ask for a retraction.

Worse are ministers — and Baird is a frequent offender — who read a quote and then whip their colleagues into a frenzy by asking, "And do you know who said that?" Backbenchers then respond enthusiastically with juvenile choruses of "Who?" This little bit of theatre is repeated several times to the great glee of Conservative members, until the minister points across the floor, celebrating a quote from a member of an opposition party: "That's who!" We're a long way from the oratory of Winston Churchill.

While the questions and answers themselves become more infantile, the more egregious behaviour is the disrespectful heckling and haranguing of members who have the floor. There has always been a certain amount of background noise, thumping of desks and "here, heres" in parliamentary tradition, but since Stephen Harper became prime minister, it has become vile. No party has a perfect record for civility. The most respectful and on point is the Bloc Québécois. The NDP is worse than the Bloc, but rarely as bad as the Liberals. The Liberal caucus has members with a tendency to heckle, but they look like Little Lord Fauntleroys next to the Conservative benches.

This is ironic, as the CPC's roots have less connection to the previous Progressive Conservative Party than to the Reform Party. And it was Reform founder and former leader Preston Manning who tried most visibly to have a policy of zero tolerance for heckling. Years later he recalled that this initiative failed simply because the media did not cover their work as a civil opposition party.[25] The heckling and the rudeness got more ink.

Liberal MP Carolyn Bennett was also resolved never to heckle in the House. As a medical doctor, feminist, and professional woman, she considered it degrading even to consider heckling across the floor. Nevertheless she found she could not function in that atmosphere without returning the shouts from the other parties.[26]

Heckling has become much more common over the last two decades or so. And the collective forgetting that there was ever a time when the House was typified by a greater level of civility makes it hard to explain the ways in which it has now become far worse.

One unpleasant aspect to the current heckling is the willingness of the government front benches to engage in rude shouting across the floor. Bad behaviour used to be reserved for backbenchers who tended to remain rather anonymous in their interruptions. Even when such opposition heckling was notorious, as in the case of the famous Liberal "Rat Pack," it was by a scattering of MPs, not by an entire caucus and rarely, if ever, by government ministers.[27] Under the current government, a number of ministers will initiate heckling across the floor. The prime minister himself does not stoop to it, although it is clear that he encourages a pit bull approach from his ministers on certain files. The decision to assign the role of lead on a number of controversial files, not to the minister in question, but to aggressive and belligerent MPs, like Pierre Poilievre, who handled the "In-Out Scandal" in Question Period, and Peter Van Loan, who as House leader in the first Harper government took many questions away from responsible ministers, suggests Harper's preference for aggressive partisanship in the House. From my observation, some ministers in the first Harper government never stooped to heckling: Jim Prentice, Tony Clement, Chuck Strahl, Gordon O'Connor, Monte Solberg, and Rob Nicholson. However, Vic Toews, Peter MacKay, Maxime Bernier, John Baird, Peter Van Loan, and Jim Flaherty often acted like bad boys in grade school.

Who else but bad boys in grade school would have found the following parliamentary behaviour clever? In one memorable Question Period, the question was about the safety of pet food in response to the tragic incident of poisoned pet food from China. The Conservative backbenchers started barking, "Woof, woof. Bow-wow." Since that day, my daughter has refused to accompany me to Question Period. She just finds it too depressing.

Heckling has also taken a crueler tone. Sexist taunts are more common. Government MPs have even taken to loud booing of certain Liberal MPs they most dislike, even before a question can be asked. This is particularly the case for women MPs. For a while, whenever Judy Sgro rose to speak, the Conservatives would chant "pizza" in reference to the allegations from a campaign worker that she had violated elections laws by accepting free pizza for her volunteers. Although she was cleared by Elections Canada, chanting "pizza" seems to entertain the Conservatives.

Some of the worst examples are well known, such as the time Peter MacKay referred to Liberal MP Belinda Stronach as a dog. I was in the House that day. The Speaker has agreed to give me a reserved seat in the front row of the diplomatic gallery. This places me directly opposite the Speaker on a second-floor balcony. I can see nearly all the MPs very clearly, but I can rarely hear well above the roar. The Commons chamber has challenging acoustics and each seat is equipped with headphones to follow the proceedings. Simultaneous translation (English–French) is provided. As the headphones carry the voice only of the person speaking into the microphone, it is almost impossible to hear clearly the words used by hecklers.

A question had been put to the government about the delay in passing amendments to the Criminal Code to punish more seriously acts of cruelty to animals. One of the Liberals' more aggressive hecklers, David McGuinty, got into a debate across the floor with Conservatives. He clearly called out to Peter MacKay words to the effect of "Don't you love your dog?" I saw Peter's gesture clearly. He pointed to the seat reserved for Belinda Stronach, who was absent that day, and shouted something. As most Canadians know, Peter MacKay had been involved romantically with Belinda Stronach when she was in the Conservative Party.

When she crossed the floor to join Paul Martin's Liberal government in spring 2005, Peter MacKay played the role of jilted lover for all the national media to see. Tellingly, Stronach never spoke of her personal relationship with MacKay, keeping private the likely scenario that he broke off their relationship when she changed parties.

When Peter MacKay shot back his retort at David McGuinty, there was a palpable reaction. It is always clear when an MP has crossed the line. The faces around the offender register shock, even if the words aren't audible. Sometimes what male Conservative MPs say is so bad that their female colleagues turn to scold them. In this case, the women journalists just above the Speaker, and thus much closer to Peter MacKay's seat than I was, also looked shocked. It was later reported that he had said, "You've got her." MacKay made things worse by denying the remark.

My conclusion is that the atmosphere in Question Period has become so disgraceful that people who would not ordinarily be crude are egged on by colleagues and become the worst version of themselves.

Far worse abuse was routinely heaped on Belinda Stronach. I honestly do not know how she withstood the attacks to remain as MP throughout her elected term. When the media reported she was romantically involved with Canadian hockey star Ty Domi, Conservative MPs would start chanting, "Domi! Domi! Domi!" every time she rose to speak.

Glen Pearson, Liberal MP from London North Centre, has complained that the atmosphere in the House constitutes abuse. School groups leave their planned field trip early as teachers hustle their charges away from the scene of our government at work. Canadians long for a Parliament that respects the institution, democracy, and each other. "Government by thunderbolt" with a prime minister who makes all the key decisions is not the Westminster tradition. We must find our find our way back to a level of debate that moves issues forward and allows government to function as it should. And we must relearn how to do it with civility.

There are roadmaps. The April 2008 report of the Centre for the Study of Democracy at Queen's University, "Everything Old Is New Again: Observations on Parliamentary Reform," summarized Canada's parliament as "executive-centred, party-dominated, [and] adversarial-minded."[28] Bearing that in mind, the study sets out some sensible approaches to reform Parliament to benefit from greater accountability, more strategic use of public policy experts and citizen dialogue, reform of political parties to ensure improved education and research capacity, as well as through a more meaningful role for independent MPs. It is a reasonable, incremental approach to improve the functioning of Parliament. We just need a government that cares to reverse, rather than accelerate, dangerous trends towards autocracy.

Chapter 3

The Americanization of
Our Election Process

Just as our parliamentary system has been absorbing aspects of U.S.-style "presidential" government, but without its compensatory checks and balances, so too has our political culture been contaminated with the aggressive dumbing down of political discourse that had been the norm south of the border up until the 2008 election.

Increasingly, our government tracks issues for short-term advantage. Decisions are made on the basis of public opinion research far more than on the basis of policy analysis by the civil service. The use of polls has grown over the years and was already having an influence on governments decades ago.[1] Finding out what the public wants and delivering is not antidemocratic. Initially, governments polled to find out if their policies would be well received by the public. When polls showed, as they did in the late 1980s, that environment was the top concern of the majority of

Canadians, governments responded with a greater priority on environmental solutions. The worrying trend is the focus on using polls to manipulate public opinion. For example, finding out that the majority of Canadians want action on climate, which we do in large numbers, and then committing to reductions in greenhouse gases is valid. But public opinion research and focus groups are increasingly used to "sell" Canadians something they do not want. They are employed by governments to find out what messages will work so that they can *avoid* doing what people want.

In the 1993 election campaign, the use of tax dollars to track public opinion for partisan purposes became an election issue. Liberal Leader Jean Chrétien pledged that, if elected, he would reduce the amount of money spent on such polling.[2] Whereas in the first year of the Mulroney government, $14 million had been spent on polling, the Chrétien government boasted it had cut this to $4 million, but over the Liberals' ensuing years in office expenditures on focus groups and opinion research began to climb. By 1994–95, Chrétien's spending was up to $7 million.[3] By 2004–05, the Paul Martin government had more than doubled the previous Mulroney record. Spending on polling was up to $29 million.[4]

In the 2006 election campaign, the Conservatives attacked the Martin government on this issue. It fit neatly into their "Liberal culture of entitlement" narrative. Yet, once in government, the Harper Conservatives managed to top even the Liberals' level of spending. In 2006–07, the federal government spent more than $31 million on polls.[5] What is all this polling for?

Well, it's certainly no longer about simply testing public opinion on issues. It is increasingly designed to find out what predictable responses will come from segments of the public. Research is targeted to know what messages appeal to young single women and what appeals to middle-aged dads. Public opinion research, including analysis from focus groups, can then be matched to the kind of marketing expertise that allows McDonald's to sell the latest full-meal deal.

The precision within the Conservative database exceeded anything available to political parties in the past. In fact, under Stephen Harper, the use of databases detailing voter intentions and inclinations has become a science. According to *Globe and Mail* journalist Michael Valpy, the Conservatives have perfected a database over a four-year period that rivals any previous efforts by any party. Of one aspect, called FRAN, Valpy writes:

> The Conservatives have enlisted neighbourhood leaders
> – sports team coaches, community activists – to report
> information on voters to the party's data collectors and
> introduce potential supporters to party campaigners, a
> technique known by its acronym of FRAN: Friends,
> Relatives, Acquaintances and Neighbours . . .

> They have assembled their voter data through
> geo-demographic and psycho-demographic surveys,
> huge-sample polling and personal contacts made with
> voters through direct mail, e-mail, telephone calls
> and FRAN contacts.[6]

This database is how the Harper Conservatives identified voters who were supposedly Jewish and mailed them Rosh Hashana cards. Valpy goes on to say:

> Political strategists say it is enabling the Tories to run
> the most micro-targeted campaign the country has ever
> experienced, aimed at favoured ethnic and cultural
> groups – Chinese, South Asians, Jews – economically
> beleaguered "battlers" and a broad spectrum of "aspi-
> rational voters" wanting more material gains for
> themselves and their children and feeling ripped off
> by the state, the elites and big business.[7]

The analysis – riding by riding – of the prejudices, likes, and dislikes of specific types of voters in key ridings sets the priorities for government. No longer is government content with knowing what the majority of Canadians would like to see; the Conservative database lets the party know what key messages and token policies will shift their vote in individual ridings. Policy is trumped by non-stop electioneering.

A good example is the cut to the GST advocated by the Conservatives in the 2006 election and then executed by the Harper government. Every economist in the country and every columnist in the pages of every business section of every newspaper railed against GST cuts. The overwhelming opinion of both academic and business economists was that cuts were needed in income tax and payroll taxes to stimulate the economy, and that all a GST cut would do would be to deprive the central government of much-needed revenue. So too were "boutique tax cuts" decried by economists, such as the Harper government's tax deduction for the fees paid by parents who enroll their children in qualifying sports or recreational activities.

This kind of very targeted tax cut was not good policy, but it was good politics. And it was based on the political strategies of the right-wing Liberals of Australia and of the Republicans south of the border

Canadian elections are still a far cry from the spectacle of American campaigns. The U.S. presidential election process now begins two years in advance of the November vote. The road to 1600 Pennsylvania Avenue is excruciatingly long and punishingly expensive.

Federal Election Commission Chairman Michael E. Toner estimated the total costs of all candidates in the 2008 election campaign would hit an all-time record of $1 billion. Furthermore, to be a legitimate contender requires a candidate to raise a minimum of $100 million. Both Barack

Obama and Hillary Clinton raised millions of dollars a week just to keep their electoral hopes alive. Unlike Canadian elections, where new financing rules brought in by Prime Minister Jean Chrétien forbid donations from corporations, unions, or any organization, U.S. elections are driven by vast pools of funds from interest groups and corporations. These are called Political Action Committees and PAC money can drive the agendas of parties. Under the *Federal Accountability Act* (2007), brought in by Prime Minister Stephen Harper, the maximum personal donation to a political party in Canada is $1,100 per year, whereas U.S. election laws permit millions of dollars in personal donations.

Canadian elections have blessedly brief, even overly brief, campaign periods. There is no equivalent to the primary season, and it would be unprecedented if the major federal parties ever had leadership races at the same time.[8] Leaders are selected by their respective parties and party leadership is rarely in doubt when the writ is dropped. A famous exception, of course, was the 1980 election, when the Liberals brought down the Progressive Conservative minority government of Joe Clark. Although Pierre Trudeau had resigned the leadership in 1979, a wily Allan J. MacEachen persuaded him to return, and the Liberals went on to win the election.

The relative simplicity and small number of people involved in selecting a leader of a Canadian political party is a weak spot in our democracy. It used to be possible for monied influence outside Canada to push the country into directions favourable to their own agendas, and to dislodge one political leader and install another. This scenario may sound far-fetched, but evidence suggests that is exactly what happened when Brian Mulroney campaigned to replace Joe Clark as leader of the Progressive Conservative Party in the early 1980s.

The testimony of Karlheinz Schreiber to the House Ethics Committee in 2008 included the remarkable admission that he had funnelled money from a consortium of wealthy conservative Europeans to the Mulroney campaign. Schreiber, who has been linked to shady efforts in lobbying with alleged kickbacks to Canadian politicians, claimed he had delivered funds to politicians in many countries in the hopes of displacing moderate leaders with more hard-line right-wing candidates. In order to ensure that Joe Clark fell short of his self-imposed vote of confidence threshold of 70 percent at the January 1983 Winnipeg convention, $370,000 in foreign money had paid for travel and hotels for a new base of pro-Mulroney Quebec delegates.[9]

Fortunately, current election rules prohibit contributions to leadership races from foreign sources. But such rules were not in place when Stephen Harper won the Alliance leadership. Harper has been asked repeatedly to reveal the list of his donors in that leadership race. No law requires him to do so, and he has refused.

The U.S. election cycle is as immovable as the cycles of the moon. Elections for president take place on the first Tuesday of November every four years. In Canada, as we well know, the timing of elections is the subject of much speculation, most of it wrong, and despite Harper's famous fixed election date law, about as predictable as a roulette wheel.

Despite our differences, the tone and style of U.S. politics have begun to dominate in Canada. There have been more negative attack ads, more electioneering outside of a writ periods, and a "take no prisoners" approach to politics that succeeds in turning voters off the process. The term "war room" was coined by Bill Clinton's brilliant strategist James Carville. Canadian politicos followed that lead. We now have war rooms too, and they are armed year-round. At the launch of the 2008 campaign, reporter David Akin wrote, "Harper paid a visit to these folks [the 100 staff in his campaign HQ] to pump his troops up as he and they head into battle for the Oct. 14 vote."[10] Democracy as war: the metaphor may be appropriate, but the culture it creates is profoundly antidemocratic.

The ultimate power and control centre, the war room, was ready and loaded by Stephen Harper's Conservatives a year and a half before the writ was dropped for the 2008 election.[11] The Liberals dubbed it a "fear factory." The 17,000-square-foot battle station occupied the entire second floor of an office building in Ottawa's east end. On

April 2, 2007, it was displayed to reporters in a salvo of pyrotechnic sabre-rattling that was the equivalent of a communications "shock and awe" campaign:

> The campaign headquarters, considerably larger than the base used by the Conservatives in the last election, includes a television studio, training facilities and a war room. In the main strategy room, workstations with flat-screen computers have been set up for everything from "candidate support" to "direct voter contact."
>
> The walls are blanketed with posters of Harper.
>
> If an election is called, the Conservatives could fire up a campaign almost instantaneously, party officials say.[12]

Conservative attack ads were rolled out nearly two years before the election was called. The advent of attack ads in Canada started well before the Harper Conservatives, however. The first negative television ad was a Liberal one in 1980 that was highly critical of Joe Clark's Conservatives. By today's standards it was uplifting and edifying. The only thing about it that made it an "attack" was that it focused on criticizing Clark's policies instead of putting forward the Liberal platform.

Since then the use of televised ads to criticize political opponents has grown in Canada. Canadians are not generally fond of such ads. Media pundits have debated for years the risks of "going negative." In fact, a misguided attack ad in the 1993 election contributed to the near shutout of the Progressive Conservatives. A Tory ad featured a close up of Jean Chrétien's slight facial palsy, suggesting that a physical defect made him unfit to be prime minister. Prime Minister Kim Campbell pulled the ad quickly and apologized. Communications gurus in recent years have suggested she made a mistake and should have let the ad run and defended it because it might have worked, just as the Harper campaign's ads against Stéphane Dion did in 2008. Either way, Canadians formed a negative impression of Campbell as a result of her party's efforts to ridicule Chrétien's physical handicap.

Meanwhile, south of the border, it seems that no ad is off limits, no matter how mean-spirited or inaccurate. In 1988, Democratic presidential nominee Michael Dukakis faced a barrage of attack ads. The one that may have done him the most damage featured a revolving door, suggesting that as governor of Massachusetts he had allowed prisoner Willy Horton to go on a killing spree by signing a routine weekend furlough. Republican George H.W. Bush won the White House.

Democratic nominee John Kerry lost the race in 2004 largely due to an aggressive campaign to demolish one of his major strengths – his war record. In 1971, Kerry had made headlines and his reputation when, as a returning war hero from Vietnam, he had thrown his war medals over a fence at the Capitol. Kerry joined Vietnam Veterans Against the War and testified about the futility of the war before a Senate Committee. His question "How do you ask a man to be the last man to die for a mistake?" was an iconic moment in the campaign to end the war. His record for heroism culminated in his election to the Senate and his gaining the Democratic presidential nomination. The third-party ads attacking Kerry went right after his war record. He had captained a naval vessel called a "swift boat" during the war. When a mine blew up near his boat, despite being wounded himself, he pulled one of his men back into the boat. He received the Purple Heart and a Bronze Star for bravery. In the television ads, former members of his battalion were featured denying he had been brave, claiming his heroism was a myth. The ads were so effective that *swift boat* went from noun to verb in politics. To be "swift-boated" came to mean having your reputation demolished. Everyone in the political game was pretty sure the ads were lies, but that didn't matter. They were effective.

George W. Bush's destruction of Kerry's campaign was at least partially the result of advice from U.S. pollster Frank Luntz. Luntz is the Republican spin doctor who advised the Bush campaign to label Kerry as indecisive with the euphonious epithet "flip-flopper." Bush called Kerry a flip-flopper in his convention speech and then followed up with attack ads and loads of help from a compliant media.

When Kerry entered the Ohio primary, Luntz polled swing voters to find out what one word they would use to describe John Kerry. The overwhelming response was "flip-flopper." Canadian journalist Donald Gutstein confirmed the framing of Kerry through a simple experiment: "Google 'John Kerry' and 'flip flop' and you'll get 250,000 hits."[13]

The campaign to re-elect Stephen Harper sought out Luntz's advice early in their planning.[14] In May 2006, just four months after Conservative victory, Luntz addressed a core group of two hundred Harper supporters at a Montreal meeting of the Civitas Society, including then chief of staff Ian Brodie and senior campaign advisor Tom Flanagan.

The Harper campaign also relied on U.S. Republican strategist Mike Murphy, who offered advice on how to "slice and dice the demographic segments." His expertise used the FRAN database system to great effect. While Luntz and Murphy played a role in the 2008 Conservative strategy, Michael Valpy has argued that Australian advisors were even more influential. "They have also lifted their campaign strategy holus-bolus from the people who fashioned the four electoral victories of John Howard's right-wing Liberal government in Australia from 1996 to 2004," wrote Valpy.[15]

The electioneering style of John Howard in Australia mastered the political art of framing opponents in an unflattering light. The Howard government also specialized in the token symbolic gesture, similar to Harper's GST cuts. Australian media reported that the reason for the

$16,925 flight to Australia in May 2007 by Ian Brodie, former chief of staff to Prime Minister Harper, was to thank Howard for his campaign help.[16] And John Howard was the first foreign head of government to visit Canada after Harper was elected.

The Howard and Bush campaigns had set a standard for Stephen Harper when it came to ruthless campaigning. Following their example, the Harper Conservatives elevated the use of attack ads in Canada. The election financing rules apply only during the writ period, or once an election has been called. There are no rules to cap spending on advertisements between elections. Running paid political television ads well before an election, as the Conservatives did in early 2007, was a stunning departure from normal political practice. The ads attacking Stéphane Dion hit the airwaves in the period closely following the December 2, 2006 Liberal convention at which he won the leadership.

After the Christmas holidays Dion was likely expecting something of a media honeymoon. He would have had one if not for the barrage of "Dion: Not a Leader" ads. The first ads hit with large buys in prime time in January 2007. With clips from the Liberal leadership debates, the ads featured an exchange between leadership rivals Michael Ignatieff and Stéphane Dion. Not an effective campaigner in English at the best of times, Dion's response in debate was damaging. When attacked by Ignatieff who charged that Dion "didn't get the job done" on Kyoto, Dion protested, "That's not fair . . . Do you think it is easy to make priorities?" Having watched Dion closely as environment minister, I never thought he had any problem "making priorities." Struggling with a second language, as I do in French, I am convinced Dion intended to say that "achieving priorities" is difficult, not making them. The French verb "to do," which is *faire,* could mean either "achieve" or "make" in English.

The Liberals did not respond with counterattack paid advertising. Dion apparently rejected advice that he should fight back, remaining convinced that Canadians were so fair-minded that voters would see through the CPC ads. In some ways, he was right, but that did not make the ads less damaging.

Next the Conservatives bought a highly prized ad placement during the February 4 Super Bowl game. In an intense campaign that must have cost many millions of dollars they sought to define the little-known former minister of environment before Canadians could get to know him themselves. At the time Jason Kenney, then secretary of state for multiculturalism, spoke about the Conservative strategy: "We want to demonstrate the only thing green about Stéphane Dion is his inexperience as a leader. You'll be seeing these ads on shows a lot of people watch. We're just looking for high exposure to our message."[17]

By mid-February, yet more attack ads were launched against Dion. These ones in French attempted to link him to the sponsorship scandal of the Chrétien government, even though, as reporters noted, he had been absolved of any knowledge or connection to the scheme by the commission investigating the matter.[18] In early April a fourth wave of attack ads hit, these also aimed at undermining Dion in his native Quebec. The ads trumpeted the funds for Quebec in Harper's new budget and included a clip of Dion stating the fiscal imbalance was a myth.[19]

There was no respite. By late May a fifth round of ads – some for television, some on radio, and a new website – all took aim at Dion, ridiculing him and attacking the Liberals in the Senate for slowing down Conservative legislation.[20] Bernie Gauthier, an Ottawa media consultant, told CTV: "Why they work is that they basically put the other leader on the defensive, so they make it very hard for a new leader like Stéphane Dion to emerge and say 'this is what I stand for' . . . Instead, he has to respond to a series of attack ads, which puts him at a real disadvantage."[21]

All in all, the Conservative Party ran a series of six attack ads characterizing Dion as an ineffectual flip-flopper between January 2007 and when they brought down their own government in September 2008.[22] As the dismal parliamentary session ground on, the Conservative ads ate up millions of dollars of free air time. All the Harperites had to do was tell the media about their plans and the ads ran as news items for free. The attack ads in June were destined for gas station screens. They featured a talking oil drop and were broadcast by the news media all over Canada, even though it turned out that the gas station chains they were meant for were unwilling to sell space for political ads.

As Steven Maher wrote in a post-campaign analysis in the Halifax *Chronicle Herald:* "By now, it is almost Pavlovian. When you say the words 'Stéphane Dion,' the first thought to pop into your head is 'not a leader.'"[23]

In his statement resigning leadership of the Liberal Party, Stéphane Dion identified the attack ads as fatal to his chances, warning future Liberal leaders that they must never allow the Harper Conservatives to define them before they could define themselves.[24]

The common wisdom is that negative advertising works. But how does it work?

The answer from the 2008 campaign is troubling for democracy. The ads worked, but they worked by discouraging people from voting. According to Angus Reid Strategies, the respected polling firm, the ads caused some Liberals not to vote for their party and resulted in even more Canadians becoming so disgusted that they did not vote at all.[25] In fact, an ad that focused on a hand throwing dice, calling a vote for Dion a gamble, all on its own persuaded 11 percent of Canadians not to vote.

The 2008 election hit an historic low for voter turnout. Only 58 per cent of Canadians voted, compared with 72 percent in 1993. "We're obviously disappointed by voter turnout," Stephen Harper said. "It's low and been getting lower for some time now." As journalist Steve Maher pointed out, "Mr. Harper is not at all disappointed that more people didn't vote in this election, since he has been working diligently for almost two years to make sure that the Liberals stayed home."[26]

When pundits and strategists claim "attack ads work," they mean it in the most cynical of terms. As Ipsos Reid researcher Andrew Grenville told the *Vancouver Sun:* "Attack ads can often work in the short term. They can give you a short boost. But they reduce the number of people who want to vote. They reduce participation in the democratic process. They poison the system."[27]

Elections should be about issues and ideas. The debates should focus on policy and solutions. It has been a long time since that was the case. In the 1993 campaign, Kim Campbell famously said that an election is not the time to explain complex policy.[28] She was eviscerated for her remark, but its truth was indisputable. The media are not interested in issues during a campaign, but in lost luggage and dropped footballs, missed questions and sweater vests. Somehow the media lose track of the issues and treat an election campaign as something between a horse race and a beauty contest.

Little wonder that the dumbing down of political discourse, the attack ads and war rooms reign triumphant. The fifth estate is an enabler in this addiction to political trivia in place of reasoned debate.

Chapter 4

Democracy and the Media

FREE SPEECH AND FREE AND FULL ACCESS to critical information are essential to democracy. As Thomas Jefferson said, "The price of freedom is eternal vigilance."

That vigilance has traditionally been vested in a free media. From Thomas Paine's Common Sense handbills to the muckraking of Bob Woodward and Carl Bernstein, the news media can function as a check on the exercise of raw political power.

The essence of a healthy news media is diversity and independence. Any democratic society needs a range of independently owned newspapers and electronic media. Concentration of ownership and corporate control have visited a disaster on the American news media. Fox News effectively acted as the house organ of the Bush administration. With General Electric controlling NBC, can that network properly cover the military-industrial complex?

Since entertainment moguls began taking over networks, there has been a perceptible loss of meaningful journalism. American media columnist Howard Kurtz has said, "There is a cancer eating away at the news business – the cancer of boredom, superficiality, and irrelevance – and radical surgery is needed." [1]

The replacement of content with celebrity, of issues with trivia, has left the world's most powerful nation with a population that doesn't know its history or that of others. One wag has said that the reason the United States goes to war is to teach its citizens geography. The media obsession with the (literal) trials and tribulations of celebrity figures like O. J. Simpson, Michael Jackson, and Britney Spears speaks to a dramatic loss of relevance for journalism in a democracy.

Canadians tend to be smug; we have the CBC after all. But we have been snoozing while the ownership of the Canadian news media has been increasingly centralized in interlocking near-monopolies and funding to the CBC has been slashed. In both private media companies and the CBC, reporters have been sacked, content has been diminished, and the corporate monoliths have interfered in elections in ways that would make Fox News blush.

David Taras, a Canadian academic teaching at the University of Calgary, has documented these trends in *Power and Betrayal in the Canadian Media:*

> Newspaper ownership has fallen into the hands of a small handful of individuals . . . and the quality of journalism has deteriorated. Our local newscasts and front pages are dominated by blood-and-gore crime stories, celebrity news, sports hype, and the latest tidbits from the world of entertainment, while reports about political and social policies rarely grab the spotlight unless they feature high-octane confrontation or pathetic victims.[2]

Canada once had a lot of strong independent newspapers. Small towns and cities boasted extremely high-quality journalists and newspapers. The *Peterborough Examiner,* the *London Free Press,* Kingston's *Whig Standard,* and the *Windsor Star* are all examples of newspapers that employed diligent reporters who broke major stories. Icons of Canadian literature were associated with such papers. Robertson Davies once was the publisher of the *Peterborough Examiner,* and his nephew Michael Davies was the superb publisher of the *Whig Standard.* In 1970, the *Windsor Star* endorsed the New Democratic Party in a federal election campaign – the first major paper to do so. Paul McKay at the *Whig Standard* wrote a series in the 1980s on the nuclear industry and contributed to a far higher level of public awareness of its risks. For this and other pieces, McKay won a string of journalism awards. But one by one, these papers and others have been absorbed into larger chains, had their workforces cut, and a large portion of their content supplied by corporate owners, with an attendant loss of local content and a diminishment in the quality of their reporting.

The threat of media concentration of ownership is not new. It first surfaced in Canada as a matter of concern in 1969 when Senator Keith Davey chaired the Special Senate Committee on Mass Media. The committee concluded that "this country should no longer tolerate a situation where the public interest, in so vital a field as information, is dependent on the greed or goodwill of an extremely privileged group of businessmen."[3]

The Davey Committee report warned of the dangers of media monopolies and urged the creation of a press council to operate at arm's length from government. The council's mandate would be to review every proposed merger to see if it could be justified in the public interest. Press councils were formed in the wake of the report and at this writing exist in every province except Saskatchewan. They deal primarily with citizen complaints, as the reforms were too weak to deal with the growing power of media concentration. The Davey Report was clear that the presumption was against the benefit of mergers: "All transactions that increase concentration of ownership in the mass media are undesirable and contrary to the public interest unless shown to be otherwise."[4] As one independent newspaper owner put it to the committee: "Diversity of opinion and aggressive newsgathering tend to disappear with the disappearance of competition, and public opinion could thereby become more of a hostage to private interests than a master of public policy."[5]

That young newspaper owner was none other than Conrad Black, whose acquisitive nature and huge appetite for owning newspapers ended up dealing a devastating blow to independent journalism across Canada. Ironically, after failing to buy the ailing Toronto *Telegram* in 1971, Black began his takeover of small locals by using the index of the Davey Committee report. He recalled, "I picked up Keith Davey's Special Senate Committee on Mass Media Report, consulted the appendix that listed the daily newspaper owners, and telephoned all the independents, offering fairly explicitly to buy their properties."[6]

The issue of concentration of newspaper ownership received its next major investigation in 1981 with the Royal Commission on Newspapers, chaired by Tom Kent. Kent, who played a key role in Trudeau's office, was asked to head up a commission in the wake of a non-compete agreement between the Southam and Thomson chains. Thomson purchased the FP Publications Group, which owned the *Globe and Mail.* In order to keep their respective dailies alive, Thomson and Southam agreed to shut down a daily newspaper in Winnipeg or Ottawa. As a result the *Winnipeg Tribune* and the *Ottawa Journal* were closed down in September 1980.

One of the clearest expressions of the importance of

a free and independent press can be found in the opening words of the Kent Commission Report: "Freedom of the press is not a property right of owners. It is right of the people. It is part of their right to free expression, inseparable from their right to inform themselves."[7]

The Kent Commission was deeply alarmed by the level of corporate concentration of ownership in the newspapers of Canada. Ninety percent of the French-language dailies were owned by three chains, while more than 60 percent of English papers were owned by Southam, Thomson, and the Sun group. The Kent Commission described the situation as "monstrous": "Where we are is, in the Commission's opinion, entirely unacceptable for a democratic society. Too much power is put in too few hands; and it is power without accountability."[8]

Despite recommendations from the Kent Commission to reverse the trend toward greater concentration, the situation became rapidly worse. Hollinger Group under Conrad Black and business partner David Radler started a buying spree that would make Hollinger the third largest chain in the world. In 1993, Black got his first foothold in the Southam chain, buying a 22.5 percent interest, and Hollinger gained controlling interest by 1996.

When Black took over the *Windsor Star*, new management insisted on cuts of 26 percent – going from 105 news and editorial staff to seventy-eight.[9] *The Reporter* in Cambridge, Ontario experienced layoffs of 30 percent of their staff. The remaining reporters' workload doubled, from forty stories a month to eighty, plus writing editorials, working as photographers as needed, and writing opinion columns.[10] Studies by academics looked at the fate of Hollinger papers – the Regina *Leader-Post,* Montreal *Gazette, Ottawa Citizen, Vancouver Sun,* and the *Cambridge Reporter.*

In every case, they found the quality of journalism had decreased. The study on the *Leader-Post* found that the advertising content of the paper had climbed to 54 percent, with news content only 25 percent. Of the local news, 28 percent was focused on local sports. Increasing reliance on the Canadian Press wire service was supposed to make up for the loss of reporters across the industry. Canadian Press could only provide news from a national perspective and so local coverage fell off dramatically across the country. According to the Canadian Community Newspapers Association, as of February 2004, "There are eight major corporate owners in Canada that own 10 community newspapers or more each. Of the 701 community newspapers that are CCNA members, 276 are corporately owned."[11]

The change has been noticeable. In my own experience of going across the country over the last two decades offering local training sessions for grassroots activism, I have found increasingly concerned citizens were asking how they could find out what their local town and municipal councils were doing, as their actions are no longer properly covered in many newspapers. One enterprising lady told me she had asked the town clerk to email her all the agendas and motions so she could spot assaults on local heritage. Government agencies now claim everything is "open" by placing information on websites, but that puts the burden on citizens to dig through websites for provocative proposals. With fewer journalists digging into local stories there is a measurable decline in municipal government accountability.

Other media masters had the same cost-cutting preoccupation. In 1978, when *Globe and Mail* owner Kenneth Thomson brought in A. Roy Megarry as publisher, Megarry had no experience as a journalist. As an industrial accountant, he had worked in firms like Honeywell and Coopers & Lybrand and had some experience in running newspapers, coming from a stint as vice president for corporate development for the Torstar group. It was reported that Megarry announced out loud in the *Globe* newsroom, "Why do we have all these copy editors here? We pay reporters a lot of money and we expect them to get the stories right when they write them. Why don't we just use spell-checker programs?"[12]

Cost-cutting was a preoccupation of not only newspaper owners; it was a focus for television news as well. In a 2006 submission to the CRTC, Canwest asked to have CRTC requirements for local news reduced. The Canwest

MediaWorks submission explained that it was no longer committed to local TV programming, as it was "economically challenging and represents a cost center with declining return, and in many cases, significant loss."[13]

With cutbacks and fewer reporters, Canadians lost access to journalists who have a solid grasp of the issues they are covering. Respected former journalist, now Carty Chair in Business and Financial Journalism at Carleton University, Christopher Waddell made this point to a recent Senate committee hearing:

> More and more reporters are treated as general assignment reporters doing a different story each day. They may cover same-sex marriages at the Supreme Court one day, the government's plans for the Kyoto protocol the next day and federal-provincial health negotiations the day after that. In that world there is never time to develop any expertise.[14]

Meanwhile, the pace of increased media concentration has accelerated. This phenomenon is not exclusive to Canada and the United States. It is global. Rupert Murdoch controlled much of the press in Australia and the U.K., with Bertelsmann AG owning much of the German press, and so on. Conrad Black was also buying up media in other countries, in Israel and the U.K. The biggest play was in 2000 when Canwest bought up the accumulation of Black's empire in Hollinger and the Southam chain. In 2001 it added Black's national paper, the *National Post*.

Canwest Global and CTV together cover most of the country's commercial television stations and nearly all of the major English-language provincial daily newspapers. As has occurred elsewhere around the world, horizontal media conglomerates are becoming common in Canada. This means that major sources of news are now owned by the same corporations, but the links are not readily apparent to most people. The Canwest Global giant owns Global TV and its affiliates, as well as some independent affiliate television stations (CH Hamilton, Vancouver Island, and Montreal) and even a few CBC affiliates. It owns major newspapers – *National Post*, Montreal *Gazette*, Ottawa *Citizen*, all three major B.C. papers (*Vancouver Sun, The Province*, and the Victoria *Times Colonist*), the *Calgary Herald, Windsor Star*, Regina *Leader Post*, Saskatoon *StarPhoenix* and handful of other major dailies, and a few dozen community papers. The other mega-media empire is that of CTVglobemedia. It owns CTV and all its affiliates across Canada, CTV Newsnet, and the *Globe and Mail* and its publication, *Report on Business Magazine*.

Cutbacks in broadcast journalism have also been taking place. In the 1990s, CBC's budget was cut by about one third. The cuts to funding of CBC Television led to the closure of local operations across Canada. The suppertime news shows became more regional, with most stories fed in. Local CBC Television news really suffered, but privately owned networks did as well.

Media critics found fault with the federal regulator, the Canadian Radio-television and Telecommunications Commission. With so many new channels and networks being approved, the quality of Canadian programming was in decline. David Taras sums up his defence of the CBC and public broadcasting with the following: "My contention is that the economics of broadcasting and the lax standards maintained by the Canadian Radio-television and Telecommunications Commission (CRTC) have conspired to create a broadcasting system that is more Americanized and less unique and original than was the case a generation ago."[15]

In 2003, the Senate Standing Committee on Transport and Communications took up the question of media ownership as an aspect of a broad and somewhat unfocused inquiry into the Canadian news media. Initially the study was chaired by Senator Joan Fraser, but over the years the Senate Committee's work stopped and started several times. In the end, it was three years before the report was issued under a new chair, Senator Lise Bacon, who had only recently become a member of the committee. It did not zero in on any one area of concern, but took a sweeping look at several issues, from cultural diversity of reporters and newsrooms, to subsidies to magazines, weaknesses in regulation, the need for whistleblower legislation, and corporate concentration. Nevertheless, the 2006 *Final Report on the Canadian News Media* does make it clear that the issues raised by the Kent Commission and the Davey Senate Committee reports had only become more worrying over the intervening decades.

The committee found fault with regulation over media concentration. The Competition Bureau, set up under the *Competition Act,* fails to step in as media markets become monopolies. The report noted that particularly in Vancouver (Canwest dominance), Quebec francophone press (Quebecor and Gesca dominance), New Brunswick (Irving family dominance), and Newfoundland and Labrador (Transcontinental's ownership of seventeen out of twenty-one newspapers), there was a significant and worrying lack of real competition. The problem is that the Competition Bureau defines "market" as pertaining only to fair market pricing for consumers.

The Senate Committee's report noted:

> The Competition Bureau's operating procedures may be well-suited to analysing most markets for goods and services in Canada, but not the news media market. The Bureau's prescribed frame of reference — what some have called a silo approach — misses a critical dimension of news and information, namely the importance of the plurality of owners and the diversity of voices, not just in a given community but in a wider regional and national landscape.[16]

The report also found that the CRTC misses the mark. As a creature of the *Broadcasting Act,* the CRTC focuses on matters like Canadian content and cultural issues, and the musical genres of radio stations, and not on the growing problem of media concentration.

The Senate noted that the most emotional testimony focused on the problem cross-ownership in the print and electronic media. Canadian Association of Journalists National President Paul Schneidereit testified that "if you turn on the radio or turn on the TV or open a daily newspaper and they all come from the same source . . . we see that as a problem in terms of diversity."[17]

The truth of the matter is that the concentration of ownership tends to reinforce an establishment view. No government – Liberal or Conservative – has wanted to take on the issue of corporate control, because the owners tend to be the friends and power base of the parties most often in power. Despite Prime Minister Harper's extreme dislike of the Parliamentary Press Gallery, the owners of most outlets ensure he is given favourable coverage overall.

Corporate concentration and cost cutting have caused the television news on every English network in Canada to deteriorate over the last two decades. To find Canadian quality television journalism on a nightly basis, I recommend watching Radio-Canada. Contrast the length of interviews: on Radio-Canada interviews may last as long as several minutes, while English-language news outlets reduce them to thirty-second sound bites.

The lead stories in English media tend to the sensational. The horrible media catch phrase "If it bleeds, it leads" is as accurate in Canada as in the United States. The CBC's venerable *The National,* its flagship news program, falls for celebrity coverage in preference to real news content as much as any other English-language news broadcast. During the Clayoquot Sound protests in 1993, I can recall being told by a CBC reporter who had unsuccessfully "pitched" a story about the issue to *The National*'s producers that there was no room on that evening's newscast for coverage of the event due to a "big story." That night's news opened with hidden-camera footage from Princess Diana's gym.

News coverage gets even worse during elections, when the news media lose any sense for issues or solutions. A nuanced statement is an invitation to misinterpretation. Coverage has ceased to focus on substance and has shifted to treating the campaign like a horse race. The public would actually like coverage of issues, but they never get the chance. As David Taras writes: "Coverage of the 2000 Canadian federal election featured the constant reporting of polls, shrinking sound bites from the party leaders, journalists who tended to be the stars of the events they reported on, and a wholesale neglect of the major issues the country was facing."[18]

Former prime minister Kim Campbell's observation that elections may not be a good time to discuss issues may be true but not because the public isn't interested in issues. As Thomas Patterson, Harvard professor in media studies, points out, the 1992 presidential election demonstrated that the public and the media were on different wavelengths. He compared the questions asked by journalists with questions by voters. Overwhelmingly, reporters asked questions about superficial aspects of the campaign – polls, who was up, who was down, and rumours without foundation. Average citizens asked questions about real concerns – health, environment, jobs.[19] The public would welcome an approach that focused on issues, but the news media appear not to be particularly interested. They are on a 24-7 search for gaffes and blunders, real or imagined.

The 1980 federal election may be remembered more for Joe Clark's lost luggage than sensible policies advocated at the time. Any moment of failure, even when totally out of the politicians' control, such as the lost luggage, will make the news. The photo of Gilles Duceppe in a cheese factory hairnet was a source of fun and frolic, but the news media choose to ignore the question of how the Quebec party fares so well within the same federal governing system that it renounces.

Media coverage of elections has definitely gone downhill. It may be a function of group-think, twenty-four-hour news outlets that must be fed, random attacks from the blogosphere, or the fact that the top reporters in elections are political reporters who are not generally very comfortable dealing with policy details.

Another explanation comes from venerable journalist Peter Calamai. In December 2005 we were both at the 11th Conference of the Parties to the UN Framework Convention on Climate Change. The sessions were intense as participants negotiated a framework to reduce greenhouse gases to protect life on earth. Reporters were there in record numbers from all around the world. The *New York Times* reported regularly from the convention, as did the *Christian Science Monitor,* the U.K. *Guardian,* and television crews from around the world. The country that seemed to be ignoring the negotiations was Canada. This was doubly strange as not only are Canadians very concerned about the issue, but this conference took place in Montreal. The *Globe and Mail* did not bother to register a single reporter for the convention. It relied on second-hand reports from Canadian Press, represented by its excellent environmental reporter, Dennis Bueckert. The *Toronto Star* was the exception to the rule, sending both environmental reporter Peter Gorrie and science specialist Calamai. (Normally the event would have had more Canadian journalists than any other nationality, but we were in the middle of the 2006 election campaign after the minority Liberal government of Paul Martin lost a confidence vote on the opening day of the climate conference.)

The lack of coverage of the UN climate convention was at a terrible cost for the Canadian public who heard and read less about progress at the sessions than people in other countries. It was little wonder then that climate change and the Kyoto Protocol were treated as non-issues by the national news media during the 2006 election campaign.

When Prime Minister Paul Martin delivered the speech welcoming government ministers from around the world, the whole of the national media seemed to fall in line with Stephen Harper's spin doctors' misrepresentation that Martin had been undiplomatic in speaking of the responsibility of industrialized countries to fulfill their Kyoto obligations. The speech was misreported to imply that he had bluntly, and for domestic political advantage, attacked the Bush administration. In fact, Martin had received a standing ovation from the delegates. In the Canadian media he got a black eye for what should have been treated as a triumph.

Even worse was the national CBC-TV report of the speech delivered by Bill Clinton on the last day of the conference. At my invitation, the former president had come to Montreal. We have been friends for nearly forty years. His presence was controversial and the Bush administration objected, telling UN officials, "If you let Clinton in the building, we walk."

In the end, with the diplomatic assistance of the mayor of Montreal, who sponsored the former president's speech as a "side event," Bill Clinton spoke to over 5,000 people. He had not a single note in front of him and held the audience spellbound for over an hour. The weaving of science and policy was masterful. He made a clear and compelling case for climate action. Afterwards he and Paul Martin appeared at a joint news conference. The only coverage of Clinton's speech on CBC-TV's *The National* that night was an inane question from the reporter travelling on the Liberal campaign plane. Nothing about climate. Nothing about the negotiations. Just the stupidest question one could imagine: Had Belinda Stronach asked Bill Clinton for advice before she crossed the floor to join the Liberal Party?

Which brings me back to Peter Calamai. As I bemoaned the idiotic media coverage of the UN conference, he explained that when an election is called, the media "goes stupid." It is as good an explanation as I have gotten from anyone else.

Reflecting on the 2006 election, Paul Martin later recalled in his memoirs *Hell or High Water* that "British politician Enoch Powell once remarked that a politician complaining about the media is like a sailor complaining about the sea."[20] Still, he couldn't avoid criticizing the media coverage, especially of the climate convention. Martin recalled his frustration that the media ignored the policy statements and issues he hoped would be the stuff of debate.

But it is the official leaders' debates themselves that draw a lengthy complaint in Martin's memoirs. The 2005–06 campaign had four leaders' debates, two in English and two in French. Martin reveals that he had been told that questions would be asked about foreign affairs and the environment in the first debate. When they didn't come up, he was sure they'd be in the next debate. Martin writes: "Thus you can imagine my puzzlement when the issues raised in the last two were exactly the same as the first round, and there was not a single question on Canada's role in the world or the environment, both issues which were of prime concern to Canadians. Not one, in four debates."[21]

The leaders' debates are arguably the most significant democratic obligation exercised by the Canadian media during an election. This ritual is organized by the national television networks' news directors. The organizing committee refers to itself as "the Consortium" and is composed of CBC, Global, CTV, Radio-Canada, and TVA. The news crews at TVO and CPAC play no role in decision making. It was the Consortium that had told Paul Martin there would be questions on the environment and foreign policy, and the same Consortium that apparently decided against it without consulting the political parties.

The Consortium has a surprisingly large amount of discretion regarding which political party leaders will be included in the debates, the format, their number, the questions to be asked, and the issues to be addressed. Their decisions are not guided by the *Elections Act*, nor are there guidelines from any government agency. Even more peculiar is that the Consortium itself claims it has no rules or clear criteria.

In 1992, the governance of the televised leaders' debate was one of the issues canvassed by the Royal Commission on Electoral Reform. It decided against any legislation to guide the process, relying on existing broadcasting regulations and the sensible discretion of the network news heads to act in the public interest.

There have been court challenges to the media's role in running the debates and there have been CRTC rulings. The essence of the rulings thus far has been that the debates have been run in a fashion that respects the public interest. The CRTC wants to see balance and impartiality, and its deliberations have spoken of wanting to see "equitable coverage." Within that vague directive, the networks have broad discretion.

The situation is different in the United States, where a Commission on Presidential Debates was created in 1987 by the Republican and Democratic parties. It runs as a non-profit entity. The rules are clear and transparent, even if they are controversial. It effectively excludes third-party candidates, having set a threshold that third parties must have 15 percent of public support before being allowed in the debates. That said, at least it *has* rules.

Pressure is building in Canada to have a better system to run Canadian leaders' debates, and much of that pressure is a result of how I was treated during the 2008 election campaign. If any issue created excitement, it was the media frenzy and public outrage surrounding excluding me, as Green Party leader, from the debate.

In early 2007, I had been approached by then-chair of the Consortium, the editor-in-chief of CBC-TV news, Tony Burman. I had recently had a strong second-place finish in the London North Centre by-election, winning an unprecedented 26 percent of the vote for the Green Party. The decision to exclude previous Green Party leader Jim Harris from the debates in 2006 had been controversial. The idea of excluding the Greens again, after the by-election result showed us as competitive with the other parties, would be even tougher to justify. The Consortium met with us and explained that no rules excluded our participation in the debate. It was made very clear that the "rule" that a party must have a sitting MP for its leader to be allowed to participate was in fact more of a media folk tale. In fact, the Consortium asked *us* for advice. They were clearly concerned that including the Green Party might create an awkward precedent. What would they do in the future if there were a public surge for the Rhinoceros Party? What would happen if one member of Parliament declared him or herself a political party? What rules or criteria would allow the Consortium to distinguish between the circumstances that led them to agree the Green Party should be in the debates and some future circumstances for a party with a less compelling argument?

They asked the Green Party to provide some guidance. We sent them some criteria, with the suggestion that any three out of four would work as a system: one MP, and/or having a full roster of candidates across the nation, and/or being federally funded, and/or having at least 3 or 4 percent support in polls. We did not receive any clear response to our suggestion. We were told that the Consortium would not make any decision until the writ was dropped.

What we didn't know was that following that meeting the Consortium asked the Conservative Party what view it would take of having the leader of the Green Party in the debates. The Consortium was told in January 2007 that if I was included in the debates, Stephen Harper would refuse to participate. I learned about this remarkable exchange in an article by Tony Burman, published during the 2008 campaign. Burman, who had chaired the Consortium from 2000 to 2007, wrote that he felt the time had come to "pull the plug" on the Consortium's process. This is how he remembered the situation at the time of the 2007 meeting of the Consortium with the Green Party:

> Some networks worried that adding a fifth leader would make the debate "unwatchable" but we all knew that the elephant in the room was actually living at 24 Sussex Drive. And he – the Prime Minister – would effectively have veto power. Within days of the

meeting, we were privately told by the Conservative Party representative that Prime Minister Harper would not participate in the debates if the Green Party leader was there.[22]

Following Burman's departure as CBC-TV news head, the head of CTV News, Robert Hurst, became chair of the Consortium. I attempted to maintain some communication, but was never again offered a face-to-face meeting with the Consortium.

The summer was busy, as Harper called three by-elections for September 8 and one for September 22, 2008. It seemed that there was no chance of a federal election until well after those by-elections, and after the September 15 start-up of Parliament. I spent time in each of the by-election ridings, but concentrated on Guelph, where our candidate, Mike Nagy, had the best chance to win a seat.

Toward the end of August I had an overture to join the Green Party from Blair Wilson, a former Liberal MP from British Columbia who was now sitting as an Independent. As it happened I was going to be in British Columbia for a friend's wedding and arranged to spend some time with Wilson. Senior Green Party staff and I spent the day poring over his financial records and meeting with his accountant and lawyer over the allegations that had led to his leaving the Liberal Party in 2007 to sit as an Independent. By the time we sat down for dinner with Blair and his wife Kelly, it was clear that Harper was seriously considering bringing down his own government within days. Wilson sent a faxed letter to the Speaker of the House from the lounge at the Vancouver Airport on August 29, before our red-eye flight back to Ottawa. In it he officially asked to be designated as a Green Party member of Parliament.

Blair Wilson and I held a joint press conference on Saturday, August 30, 2008 at the National Press Club. It was an historical first. Media from coast to coast reported that this ensured the Green Party of Canada a place in the federal leaders' debate. Nevertheless, the party executive thought it would be wise to make sure that we delivered a gentle shot across the bow. Our past leader Jim Harris held a press conference with our counsel Peter Rosenthal, setting out the reasons that a decision to exclude us would be met with a challenge to the CRTC, and potentially to the courts as well. Later that week, I was back in Guelph campaigning with Mike Nagy. Despite ever louder drumbeats of an impending election campaign, there was still the reality that the only election that was actually set was for September 8 in Guelph and in two Montreal-area ridings.

On September 2, I was touring a local green business with Mike when I had a BlackBerry message from Robert Hurst, chair of the Consortium. He wanted me to phone immediately. Due to commitments in Guelph, I asked for a half-hour delay. The time they wanted with me shrank to ten minutes.

I joined a room full of people by speakerphone. Their names flew by faster than I could jot them down. After a blitzkrieg of questions, mostly hostile, it was over. I never heard directly from the Consortium again.

On Sunday, September 7 the prime minister visited the governor general to request an election. In so doing, he violated his own fixed election date law.

The next day, I was in Ottawa rushing from media interview to media interview, before heading back to Nova Scotia, when we heard through the grapevine that the Consortium was also meeting in Ottawa. No message on the BlackBerry. We could only hope and pray that the fact we had hit all of our criteria, and every threshold ever mentioned to us, would absolutely clinch my participation in the leaders' debate.

I reviewed the criteria in every interview. We were running over 300 candidates, coast to coast. We had a sitting MP at the dissolution of the House. While some media thought it was not good enough to have an Independent become a Green, the Bloc was initially included in the debates without any members elected as Bloc Québécois. Even Don Newman of CBC's *This Week in Politics* had not recalled that Gilles Duceppe, the first future Bloc MP to be elected in a by-election, had won his seat as an Independent. His party had not yet been legally formed. Reform was included in the debates with one MP. Deborah Grey's win in an Alberta by-election was enough to get her leader,

Preston Manning, into the debates. We had had nearly 5 percent of the vote in 2006, were federally funded, and were polling at around 10 percent of the national public opinion polls in the lead-up to the election. We thought we had covered all the bases. In order to exclude us, the Consortium would have to break with its own precedents.

At that point, we had no idea that Stephen Harper was threatening to boycott the debates if I was included. I was to find out soon. In the late afternoon on September 8, on my way in to the studio at the skyscraper offices of CTV's Ottawa's studio, I ran into Robert Hurst. I grasped his hand and asked if there was news. I think I said, "Please, Bob, you *know* we should be there." He managed to shrug slightly, disengage and not utter a syllable. A few moments later, I was in the chair in the studio of CTV's *Mike Duffy Live* news show, being taped for later broadcast. Duffy began the interview by telling me on air that I may not have seen the news release from the Consortium, but he had. I was not to be allowed to participate in the debates. Duffy said that three out of four party leaders had refused to participate if I were included. I remained calm and explained why the antidemocratic nature of the decision and the violation of fundamental fairness in the use of the public airwaves were too outrageous to allow it to stand. As I left, I told Duffy off air that I would be in the debates. The Consortium never did send the Green Party a message, nor was I ever contacted directly to explain its decision.

The decision to keep me out of the debates set off a firestorm of public protest rarely seen in Canada. The Consortium's stated explanation that three out of the four major party leaders would refuse to participate if I were included began to fall apart within minutes. It turned out not to be true, as Bloc Québécois Leader Gilles Duceppe quickly said he had not made such a threat, and neither had Liberal Leader Stéphane Dion. So that left NDP Leader Jack Layton and Stephen Harper.

The reporters travelling with Jack Layton tried to get an answer from him: was it true he had threatened to boycott the debates if Greens were included? The NDP ducked the answer for over a day until spokesperson Brad Lavigne confirmed they had made that threat. Both the Conservatives and the NDP claimed it would be like having two people arguing for the Liberal side, because Stéphane Dion and I had agreed we would not run candidates against each other in a leaders' courtesy agreement. No one knew that the Conservatives had taken that position four months before any such agreement had been contemplated.

The public reaction was unprecedented. Columnists from Andrew Coyne, traditionally conservative (who started a blog entry with, "I didn't think things could get any more Third Worldish"), to Susan Reilly, traditionally more left, called for the Consortium to reconsider. As one of Canada's most respected political journalists, Chantal

Hébert, wrote: "The Green party had a better case for participating in the televised debates of the 2008 campaign than the Bloc Québécois and the Reform party in 1993. Having opened the door 15 years ago to parties that were blatantly not in the running for power, why did the networks not stand up for Elizabeth May in this campaign?"[23]

Websites were deluged. Jack Layton's Facebook page became a forum for attacking him. The rage was surprising and very heartening. The pressure came to a head on September 10. The *Globe and Mail* had an incredibly powerful juxtaposition, with former prime minister Joe Clark on the op-ed page labelling Layton and Harper's position as "blackmail" and feminist activist Judy Rebick denouncing the NDP in a letter to the editor and stating that for the first time in her life she was ashamed of being associated with the party. Later that day in Oshawa, Jack Layton faced a spontaneous Green Party protest demanding he allow me in the debates.

Finally that same day, Jack Layton announced the "debate on the debates" was distracting people from the real issues. Within a half-hour, Conservative spokesman Kory Teneycke announced that the Conservatives no longer objected either.

The threat of a boycott was over, but the debate about the network news directors making arbitrary decisions behind closed doors was just beginning. The most authoritative voice was that of Tony Burman:

Prime Minister Harper's refusal to allow the Green Party leader to participate in the Federal Election Debates is cynical and self-serving, but at least it exposes the sham that Canada's election debate process has become.

After 40 years of relying on Canada's television networks to organize this important event, I believe it is time for Canadians – through the CRTC – to pull the plug on the networks and entrust this vital mission to an independent, non-partisan "commission" similar to how it is done in the U.S.[24]

The importance of the debates to a functioning democracy was well expressed by Burman: "This is serious business. An election is intended to protect the heartbeat of a democracy, and a televised leaders' debate is the only opportunity to see them together on the same stage. I think it's high time for an independent, non-partisan commission to step in and urgently provide remedial action."

The failure of the Consortium in this debacle hobbles any legitimacy for their independence in overseeing such an important aspect of our democracy. My experience in the debates became a sharp lesson in how the media's actions can assist one party over another.

Weeks later during the campaign, I was interviewed by Mike Duffy again. Waiting to go on air, I began to suspect that I had been deliberately set up when Duffy gave me the news that I was not in the debate, live and on air. This time I was waiting to be interviewed following a debate at St. Francis Xavier University. I had my microphone and earpiece ready to go on air by live satellite feed. Peter MacKay, whom I was hoping to unseat, was being interviewed in the segment ahead of me. Mike Duffy's introduction to Peter MacKay attempted to paint a picture of my participation in the St. Francis Xavier debate as somehow irresponsible or mentally unbalanced. While saying he didn't want to use the words "off the wall," which, of course, he just had, he went on to describe my statements in the debate as "bizarre."

It then became clear to me that Robert Hurst and Mike Duffy had planned that I find out live, on air, that I was not to be included in the debates. The way in which I was told maximized the chances of my having as unprofessional reaction as possible. An unflattering tape of my reaction could have been broadcast repeatedly to undercut the Greens' chances of being part of the debates. I realized how fortunate it was that I had been able to remain composed and articulate.

By the last weekend of the election, the use of unflattering tapes became a major factor in driving voters away from the Liberal campaign. The circumstances, just as those surrounding the debate, are likely to be the stuff of courses in journalistic ethics for years to come.

At the very end of the campaign, Liberal Leader Stéphane Dion was interviewed at a Halifax CTV affiliate,

ATV, by news anchor Steve Murphy. Murphy asked Dion a complex question involving a double hypothetical using complex verb tenses. (If he had been Prime Minister, what would he have done . . . ?) Dion started to answer and then asked if he could receive a clarification. The tenses of the question were unclear to him. "From what point would I have been prime minister? If I were prime minister today? Or a year ago?" he asked. Further requests for clarification ensued, with Steve Murphy clearly acceding. I have been in a number of situations when an interview stops and starts for retaping. It is shocking that such "outtakes" would ever see the light of day and Nova Scotia scuttlebutt has it that Steve Murphy did not want the tape used.[25] Nevertheless, CTV's *Mike Duffy Live* showed the tape, and it was played over and over again across the country in the last weekend of the campaign. There was some outcry, as some journalists asked whether this was a violation of ethics. Robert Hurst assured them that airing the tape was in the public interest. The effect was to undo any gains in public confidence that Dion had made. Using the tape was despicable, but it was effective.

The extent to which CTV created this "news story" was disturbing. Nevertheless, the *Globe and Mail* did not expose the implications of CTV's actions. Within weeks after the election a surprised Mike Duffy received a Senate appointment as a member of the Conservative caucus, leaving us to wonder if this was meant as a signal to journalists that if you help Harper you will be rewarded.

Regardless of which side of a campaign a media conglomerate favours, all Canadians should be disturbed by the fact that the quality of information reaching us has deteriorated due to layoffs and cutbacks. There is no doubt that many dedicated journalists still strive to bring effective coverage to the public, often despite the bias of the conglomerate for which they work. And the owners generally want to have some diversity of voices within their operation. Nevertheless, democracy is threatened when too few people own too many newspapers and radio and television stations. Essentially, five corporations control Canada's media, with just two, CTV Globemedia and Canwest MediaWorks, telling most Canadians what is going on. The Internet helps rebalance to an extent but not everyone uses it to follow the news. And while there are reputable and legitimate news outlets in cyberspace, there is no systematic quality control and some sites allow an irresponsible festering culture of character assassination and cruel gossip.

We Canadians think that Canada is a modern, well-informed democracy. We look down our noses at the dumbed-down content of Fox News and CNN, without noticing that we are rapidly heading in the same direction.

Chapter 5

Police State?

IN ANY HEALTHY AND FUNCTIONAL democracy, the centralization of control over the news media would be resisted. Even more so would a healthy democracy insist on keeping the state police out of politics. Of all the deteriorating aspects of Canadian democracy, the lack of concern over the ability of the national police force to interfere in elections is the one that most suggests Third World politics.

The Canadian public reveres the Royal Canadian Mounted Police. Our culture is steeped in Mountie references: They always "get their man," Nelson Eddy as the singing Mountie, Dudley Do-Right as the cartoon Mountie, the famed Musical Ride, and Paul Gross as *Due South*'s intelligent Mountie Brenton Fraser.

Few journalists take on the RCMP directly, and fewer politicians. Nathan Cullen, NDP MP for Skeena-Bulkely

Valley, is one of the few politicians to speak aloud of his concerns. In May, 2006, Cullen was frustrated with the inordinate delay in getting any answers for a bereaved mother whose son was killed in RCMP custody the previous October. Twenty-two-year-old Ian Bush was by all accounts a fun-loving normal guy, a sawmill worker in Houston, British Columbia. On October 29, 2005 he was outside the arena after enjoying a hockey game with friends when a local RCMP officer arrested him for having an open beer. As a joke he didn't give the Constable Paul Koester his real name. Koester, who had been working as an RCMP officer for five months, was not amused and took Ian Bush into custody. The last time his friends saw him alive "he was laughing, joking, in a good mood."[1]

Ian Bush was killed twenty minutes later in police custody at the lockup. He was shot in the back of the head. Seven months later, Bush's family was still waiting for answers.

Nathan Cullen – trying to get answers for Bush's mother, who is a constituent – phoned the detachment's RCMP superiors in Vancouver to ask for information. He was basically told it was none of his business. He asked whether it did not suggest the RCMP was presupposing Koester's innocence that he was still carrying a gun and working in another community.

In an interview with Gary Mason, who writes a regular B.C. column for the *Globe and Mail,* Cullen admitted there were reasons politicians were scared of criticizing the RCMP. Mason's column described Cullen's fears:

> "They say don't ever pick a fight with the police as a politician because they'll find you and show up in the middle of the night and pull your family out with television cameras and talk about that deck you had built," the NDP MP said in an interview from Ottawa.
>
> (In March, 1999, the RCMP raided the home of B.C.'s then-premier Glen Clark in connection with allegations he had helped a neighbour who had built a deck for him get a casino licence. A television station was tipped off and was there to film the raid. Mr. Clark was later cleared of any wrongdoing in the affair).
>
> Mr. Cullen went on.
>
> "The police are a significant force in our world and I'm exposed and that's the nature of my job.
>
> "But it's common parlance among politicians that taking on the police is an extremely dangerous thing to do. You can ruin your career.
>
> "You can end up completely discredited."[2]

Gary Mason's column about Cullen's fears unleashed an immediate firestorm, not directed at the RCMP, but aimed straight at Nathan Cullen. He had been right, of course, about the extraordinary way that former B.C. premier Glen Clark had been set up by the local RCMP. The television news images of Clark pacing behind closed curtains while the Mounties searched his home were as good as an episode of a reality cop show in making Clark look guilty.

In the end, the official "answers" to the Bush killing took years and answered nothing. The coroner's report came out in July 2007, and an RCMP internal investigation reported in November 2007, more than two years after Bush's death. Both the coroner and the RCMP internal investigation accepted the dubious account of the young officer. He claimed that he had killed Bush in self-defence. The officer's testimony was completely contradicted by an expert forensic investigator, Edmonton Police Services officer Joe Slemko. Slemko testified the blood splatter evidence placed Koester on top of Bush at the time the gun was fired, not under him as the officer testified. The coroner told the jury that their job was not to find fault, and thus to set aside the forensic evidence. The RCMP internal investigation by Commissioner Paul Kennedy ruled that the death was self-defence.[3]

There was also the instructive episode of Greg Sorbara's public humiliation by the RCMP. On October 11, 2005, the RCMP named the then–Ontario finance minister in search warrants related to an investigation by the RCMP white-collar crime unit. Within days, Minister Sorbara resigned, pledging to clear his name. The RCMP's Integrated Market Enforcement Team (IMET) was putting together a case related not directly to Sorbara, but to the so-called

Royal Group scandal. The allegations involved potential theft and fraud among a group of executives who made some property deals with the Sorbara family firm.

It was seven months before a judge ruled that the RCMP had had insufficient grounds for naming Greg Sorbara in the search warrant. Meanwhile, Sorbara's lawyers had been in discussions with the RCMP and the Crown since December 2005, attempting to obtain a statement that their client was not under investigation. The goal was to obtain a statement exonerating Greg Sorbara no later than February 3, to allow Premier McGuinty sufficient time to consider reinstating his former finance minister in time to prepare the provincial budget. At one point, the communication was going well. It was reported that the Crown told Sorbara's lawyers that there was not enough evidence for a prosecution.[4] This news, unfortunately for Greg Sorbara, angered the RCMP, who felt "blindsided" and blocked any further communication to Greg Sorbara's lawyers. It took the decision of Mr. Justice Ian Nordheimer of the Ontario Superior Court in May 2006 to exonerate Greg Sorbara. In a scathing review of the RCMP's conduct, Justice Nordheimer described the sketchiness of the RCMP evidence in support of a search warrant, noting that they provided no evidence of the properties in question, and further tainted some transactions in the interests of obtaining the warrant. "I am left with the nagging concern that the application for a search warrant, at least as it related to [Sorbara], was very much premature," Judge Nordheimer said.[5]

Even after that abusive process, Minister Sorbara, who was reinstated to Cabinet, was not critical of the RCMP. Despite having had to spend $100,000 to clear his name, he was magnanimous, saying, "No public organization is infallible." As Carol Goar noted in the *Toronto Star*: "Even if he is stretching the truth, Greg Sorbara is wise to say he bears no malice toward the RCMP for putting him through seven months of hell, damaging his reputation and disrupting his political career."[6]

MP Nathan Cullen's open statement of fear of the RCMP was then not without reason, but it quickly seemed unwise. He had anticipated the wrath of the RCMP for his criticisms, when he spoke to Gary Mason:

> "If I go down in a burning ball of flames [because the RCMP] pull up the fact that I got drunk in college and threw up on an officer or something and they say, 'Cullen is a drunken buffoon,' suddenly I'm no longer in the game.
>
> "Suddenly, I don't have any credibility with which to advocate. I'm done.
>
> "So I have to be smart.
>
> "It's a risk, I'll be frank about that. I know where the balance of power lies and it's not with me."[7]

Despite the fact that Cullen's statements came in exactly the same time period that Sorbara was fighting to clear his name, no one seemed prepared to defend Cullen. British Columbia Solicitor General Jon Les was enraged. He demanded that Nathan Cullen apologize.

Les is a familiar and enthusiastic defender of the RCMP. He is known for saying "We love our Mounties" so often in the provincial legislature that some joked it was his bedside prayer.[8] Even the 2007 horrific incident of RCMP officers killing a Polish immigrant with a Taser in the Vancouver Airport was not enough to move Les to action. He rebuffed any suggestion that the Province of British Columbia should conduct an independent investigation into the death of Robert Dziekanski. It was clear from the outset of his violent and senseless death at the hands of four RCMP officers that the truth would have been buried with poor Mr. Dziekanski if not for the video-taping of his final moments by another traveller. And the B.C. solicitor general was content to have the RCMP essentially investigate itself, again.

The apology for Nathan Cullen's remarks was forth-coming, but not from Cullen directly. Within days of Cullen's comments appearing in the *Globe and Mail,* NDP Leader Jack Layton apologized, saying that Cullen "regret-ted" his remarks.[9]

There is something wrong with a political culture

where elected officials are afraid of criticizing, questioning, or reprimanding the national police.

One of the few columns to pick up on this problem, David Hutton's opinion piece about the reluctance of politicians to investigate the RCMP pension scandal, appeared in *The Hill Times.* Hutton is coordinator of FAIR, the Federal Accountability Initiative for Reform:

> For decades, politicians of all stripes have shied away from taking any action: not only because they fear a backlash from the Canadian public but also because they are fearful of what could happen to them if they "take on" the RCMP.
>
> According to Shirley Heafey, former head of the Commission for Public Complaints Against the RCMP, this is not an irrational fear: she cites the devastating effects of the RCMP's actions on politicians such as Ontario MPP Greg Sorbara, and B.C. Premier Glen Clark. In these and many other similar cases the Mounties did indeed "get their man."[10]

This intimidating treatment may explain why nearly everyone in the national media and political world has turned a blind eye to the RCMP interference in the 2006 election.

The political bombshell went off in the middle of the 2005–06 federal campaign. In late December, Paul Martin's minority Liberals were leading and looked likely to gain re-election. Then, just after Christmas, Judy Wasylycia-Leis, NDP MP and finance critic, posted a letter she had received from RCMP Commissioner Giuliano Zaccardelli on her website. She had written to the RCMP requesting an investigation of allegations that some people had made stock market gains through advance knowledge of federal government's decision not to tax income trusts. "The media has reported a sharp and unusual increase of trading in income trust investments in the hours immediately preceding the Finance Minister's announcement," she wrote. "There has been speculation in the press that a leak about the government's decision could be responsible."[11] She sent this letter the day of the non-confidence vote that brought down the government, November 28, 2006. A response from the RCMP commissioner himself was sent on December 23, 2006. Ms. Wasylycia-Leis posted Zaccardelli's letter on her website on December 28, 2006.

Later that same day, the RCMP issued a press release confirming the contents of the letter Ms. Wasylycia-Leis had posted. The force was conducting a criminal investigation into the alleged leaks of insider information about the November 23 decision of the finance minister not to tax income trusts. The RCMP press release made specific mention of Finance Minister Ralph Goodale, although only to state that "at this time" they had no evidence that connected him to any wrongdoing.

The media feeding frenzy soon consumed the election campaign and destroyed Martin's chances. In a campaign that had already been framed as a referendum on whether anyone could trust the Liberal Party after the Sponsorship Scandal, a new scandal was the kiss of death. Polling numbers from late November through to just before Christmas showed the Liberals holding a lead of at least 5 percent. By early January, the situation had reversed and the Liberals never recovered.[12]

This political interference by the RCMP in an election campaign was unprecedented. Some reporters queried whether the income trust probe was "payback of some kind against the Liberals."[13] Possible motives included that the minority government of Paul Martin had launched inquiries into RCMP conduct in such illegalities as the Sponsorship Scandal and Canadian citizen Maher Arar's rendition by the United States to Syria, where he was tortured.

Some, like *Toronto Star* writer Susan Delacourt, speculated a motive born of reverse psychology — that the Mounties were tired of being accused of being too Liberal:

> Still others speculate that the national police force is sniffing the political winds, mindful of what Harper and his MPs have been alleging about the RCMP failing to go after the Liberals hard enough. Last November, when Judge John Gomery's report came out, Harper said the RCMP would have laid more charges in the

sponsorship affair if Liberals hadn't been in power. The RCMP dismisses such suggestions. It says the probes came out as part of a normal course of affairs.[14]

Staff Sergeant Paul Marsh, RCMP senior media relations officer, defended the timing of the release: "If we start adjusting the timing of our announcements, then we are becoming politicized."[15]

Following the election, there was no immediate call for an inquiry. For the defeated Liberals to have demanded one would have appeared self-serving. The NDP had played the role of willing enabler for the RCMP plan, so it was not keen to demand accountability. And Prime Minister Stephen Harper, unlike Paul Martin and his zeal to appoint Judge Gomery to uncover his own party's scandal, had no interest in investigating a scandal that had helped the Conservatives win.

On September 18, 2006, the inquiry Paul Martin had launched into the illegal rendition of Maher Arar to Syria by U.S. authorities, headed by Mr. Justice Dennis O'Connor, reported its findings. Maher Arar was completely exonerated, but the O'Connor Commission found that the RCMP had passed incorrect information about Arar to the Americans. It found that Commissioner Zaccardelli had misinformed the solicitor general both about the likelihood that Arar was tortured, as well as darkly hinting that Arar had real terrorist links. Heads should have rolled, but

Commissioner Zaccardelli kept his and he was not asked to submit his resignation when the report was issued.

Within days, there were allegations that the Prime Minister's Office and the office of Minister of Public Safety Stockwell Day had ordered the commissioner not to appear before the Commons Public Safety and National Security Committee. In the House of Commons on September 24, 2006, interim Leader of the Opposition Bill Graham repeated former RCMP Commissioner Norman Inkster's claim that Zaccardelli was being muzzled by the Harper government.[16] It was a subject of much media speculation when Zaccardelli refused to appear before the House Committee. A confidante of Zaccardelli approached the media to assert that Stockwell Day had written Zaccardelli to instruct him to avoid the House Committee.[17] The *Toronto Star* ran with the story, only to have Zaccardelli deny it. When Zaccardelli did testify in late September 2006, he said he first learned that the RCMP had made mistakes in Arar's file in 2002, shortly after Arar's deportation to torture in Syria. He also claimed he had told the government of the day that the RCMP had provided incorrect information to U.S. authorities. When former solicitor general Wayne Easter testified to the same committee on October 24, 2006, he categorically denied that the RCMP commissioner had ever told him of RCMP errors: "There is no situation where the RCMP came to me, and basically said: 'We screwed up. We provided improper information.'"[18]

The inconsistencies kept piling up. Finally in early December of 2006, Commissioner Zaccardelli told a Canadian Club audience in Ottawa that he had first learned of the significant mistakes in the RCMP's handling of Maher Arar's case only when he read Justice O'Connor's report. He had contradicted his own evidence to the House Committee of late September. Testifying once again to the House Committee on December 5, 2006, Commissioner Zaccardelli attempted to correct the record. "I believe that some aspects of my prior testimony could have been more precise and more clearly stated. A number of misconceptions have resulted," he testified. [19]

The next day, Commissioner Zaccardelli tendered his resignation and Prime Minister Stephen Harper accepted it. One columnist who did not buy the official explanation was Rick Salutin in the *Globe and Mail*:

This isn't about the Arar case, which was dealt with in the O'Connor report. It's about the last election, when the RCMP interfered in a way that led to Paul Martin's defeat and Stephen Harper's election. The force has made other gaffes, but listing them leads to under-valuing that election involvement.

In the midst of the campaign, the commissioner faxed an NDP MP, saying the Mounties were investigating then-finance minister Ralph Goodale, one of the big Liberals untinged by scandal. They don't normally do this. Nothing has come of the investigation. They could have waited. They could have kept it quiet.

Instead, they even phoned the NDP MP to say, *You've got mail*, making sure she knew it was on the way. It tipped the election. She went public, the Conservatives shot up 10 points and passed the Liberals for good. It turned the tide and led to a Harper government. I say focus on this, because it could help explain why the PM effectively protected the commish after his damaging September testimony, as if to thank him.[20]

The Harper government continued to cover for Zaccardelli even after he was no longer commissioner.

The next troubling scandal was over the misuse of RCMP pension funds. A month before Commissioner Zaccardelli resigned, an RCMP whistle-blower, Staff Sergeant Ron Lewis, sent a package to every member of the Public Accounts Committee of the House of Commons. The package documented allegations of RCMP senior officers misusing RCMP pension funds.

The scandal of the pension funds was first brought to light within the RCMP by Denise Revine in 2003. A human resources director with three decades at the force, she had been asked to review the RCMP pension and insurance plans. She uncovered a maze of sole-source contracts, kickbacks, and nepotism. She took her findings to her boss, Chief Superintendent Fraser Macaulay, who relayed them to Commissioner Zaccardelli. Zaccardelli was persuaded to begin a criminal investigation, but he put an end to it two days into the work. Cancelling the criminal investigation, Commissioner Zaccardelli ordered an internal audit instead. Staff Sergeant Lewis and Denise Revine did not let go. Three years later, they were trying to get the House Committee to look into the matter.

The members of the committee voted down proceeding with an investigation. To be more precise, the five Conservative members of the committee acted as a group to block any investigation. And they did so repeatedly from the fall of 2006 until they lost by one vote and the RCMP whistle-blowers finally appeared in April 2007.

Liberal committee member Borys Wrzesnewskyj recalled, "Every colleague I spoke to said, 'Are you sure we want to go there? Remember this is the RCMP' . . . At every key point when the committee voted to deal with the issue, they [the Conservatives] blocked it or tried to block it."[21]

The Conservative committee members also blocked pursuing reports from the auditor general that all was not well within the RCMP. In one of Don Martin's more evocative columns, he wrote of the whistle-blowers' testimony and the committee members' reactions: "It was all an act. The shock and horror displayed by MPs after the whistle-blowers implicated RCMP brass in an alleged pension fund scandal last week was indignation faked for the cameras. Unless they were wilfully ignorant, the MPs knew everything months ago. All of them."[22]

A veteran reporter possessed of an exceptionally acute mind and above-average political radar, Martin was baffled:

> It's incredible and inexplicable why a government under Prime Minister Stephen Harper, which wraps itself in the uniform of aggressive law and order, would vote repeatedly to deny RCMP officers access to the spotlight when they were willing to risk their careers telling a disquieting truth . . . there's no sensible explanation for why Conservatives, who usually act in unison in committees, would circle the wagons against RCMP insiders seeking to blow the whistle on behaviour that took place under a Liberal reign. Nor is it readily clear why Public Safety Minister Stockwell Day would order up a flaccid investigation without subpoena powers and limited to calling current RCMP staff.[23]

Or was it? A plausible explanation would be that the Conservatives still owed favours to Zaccardelli for giving them the 2006 election.

The tawdry tale of the income trust probe came to an anticlimactic end in February 2007. On February 15, the RCMP announced the findings on the criminal investigation into the alleged leaks. Charges would be laid against one relatively junior official in Finance Canada. A nearly two-year investigation established enough evidence to proceed with charges against Serge Nadeau, alleging he gained approximately $7,000 from insider information — or as Rick Salutin quipped, "For the cost of a modest kitchen renovation, a government may have lost power."[24]

At the time the RCMP announcement was made, the Conservatives were running television ads that continued to allege Ralph Goodale had done something improper. Goodale asked the prime minister for an apology. Stephen Harper rebuffed him, suggesting it was Goodale who owed an apology to the people of Canada and to the RCMP. Finance Minister Jim Flaherty and fellow Cabinet member John Baird took the same approach: no apology was required and the ads were going to continue to run.[25] "I'm not rushing to a conclusion here, but I do know one thing – those ads are false," Goodale responded. "They are being paid for by the Conservative Party, they are wrong and any decent prime minister, any decent prime minister with one modicum of integrity would do the right thing."[26]

Media commentary clearly sided with the wronged party – Ralph Goodale. The fact that Goodale, known for a squeaky-clean reputation prior to the Zaccardelli smear, had now been exonerated was ignored by the Harper government. Both Flaherty and Baird attempted to suggest that the investigation might be ongoing, and that it was possible that Goodale was still subject to an investigation.

A *Globe and Mail* editorial called for the prime minister to be more magnanimous and to both apologize and pull the ads. *Globe* columnist Jeffrey Simpson, setting the issue in the forgotten context that the Conservatives' 2006 victory "turned" on the letter from Zaccardelli, wrote, "[Goodale's] reputation was sullied by attacks from MPs, one of whom is now Prime Minister. Will anybody apologize? The question is obviously rhetorical."[27]

Even this brief media flutter failed to raise the question of what had motivated Zaccardelli to make the criminal investigation public. Finally an investigation was undertaken into the question of why the RCMP had so clearly chosen to interfere in the 2006 election. Unfortunately, it was conducted by the chair of the Commission for Public Complaints Against the RCMP. That body has no powers of subpoena, nor any ability to compel testimony.

The report of Commission Chair Paul Kennedy was released on March 31, 2008. It made several significant findings that highlighted the unprecedented personal involvement of Commissioner Zaccardelli in ensuring that the RCMP decision to launch a criminal investigation came to the attention of the media during the campaign. There was nothing routine about what took place.

It was accepted as fact by Kennedy that the RCMP letter and news release had caused the swing in public opinion that cost the Liberals the election. In tracing the chronology, Kennedy found that a meeting had taken place on either December 21 or 22, at which Commissioner Zaccardelli "decided to write a letter to Ms. Wasylycia-Leis advising that a criminal investigation had been commenced. He indicated that he would sign and send the letter."[28]

With the letter prepared for his signature on December 23, Commissioner Zaccardelli was very insistent that it be sent without delay. The commissioner instructed Superintendent Mike McDonald, his executive assistant, to make sure it was faxed. At approximately 3:15 P.M. on December 23, McDonald checked with Judy Wasylycia-Leis's offices on Parliament Hill and with her constituency office in Winnipeg. Both offices had a taped message that they were closed for the holidays and would reopen January 3, 2006. Rather than simply fax the letters and await their discovery in the New Year, McDonald left messages at both offices that a letter was being faxed and then did so.

There is no public account of the reaction in Wasylycia-Leis's office when the late Christmas present was discovered. It is a fair assumption that if it had been discovered the day it was faxed, it would have been posted on her website without delay. When it made its public debut December 28, 2006, Commissioner Zaccardelli took the unusual step of issuing a press release confirming the letter. It is the evidence of Public Complaints Commission that it was Commissioner Zaccardelli who wanted a press release issued in response to media calls. Short-staffed over the holidays, Acting Director of Corporate Communications Nancy Sample prepared a draft release. It did not include the names of any suspects. The draft was rejected and Sample was told, "The Commissioner requested Mr. Goodale's name be added."[29]

Nancy Sample sent two versions of the press release to the commissioner's office – one mentioning Ralph Goodale and one that did not. "Commissioner Zaccardelli approved the version containing Mr. Goodale's name, and the press release was issued."[30]

RCMP complaints commission chair Paul Kennedy notes in his findings that the treatment of Wasylycia-Leis's letter was unusual. While he found there were no specific guidelines for situations such as these, under normal RCMP guidelines a complainant is entitled to be "apprised of progress" so long as there is no "injury, injustice or embarrassment to the victims of the accused." RCMP guidelines further state that *the names of suspects should never be released prior to charges being laid* "(emphasis added).[31] Kennedy's report notes, "Here, Ms. Wasylycia-Leis, although merely reflecting media speculations, was elevated to the status of a complainant and was provided with written confirmation of the criminal investigation."[32]

On the face of it, Kennedy makes it clear that Commissioner Zaccardelli had violated RCMP guidelines. There was no need to treat the NDP finance critic as a complainant and it was a further violation to name a suspect,

Ralph Goodale. It was even more egregious to do so in a press release in the middle of a federal election campaign.

Having made all the links to existing guidelines which Commissioner Zaccardelli violated, Paul Kennedy's report stopped short of saying so. In the "Findings" section of his report, he states that the RCMP have no policies for "the public release of information in highly sensitive situations such as that existing in his instance . . . Given the absence of any such specific policy, procedure or guideline, I cannot find that any RCMP officer failed to comply with applicable standards."[33] The mind boggles at the notion that the violation of routine guidelines to keep investigations out of the public view and not to reveal the names of potential suspects prior to the laying of charges was made moot by the fact it was exceptionally sensitive information.

Even more provocative was the fact that the entire public complaints commission investigation had to make do without the testimony or any statement from the key player. Former Commissioner Zaccardelli refused to be interviewed or to provide a statement. Paul Kennedy noted:

> In light of his refusal to provide a statement, it is impossible to determine what factors former Commissioner Zaccardelli may have considered in support of his decision to write the letter of December 23rd nor the particular urgency to communicate to Ms. Waslylcia-Leis the change in status from review to criminal

> investigation. However, *there is no evidence that*
> *Commissioner Zaccardelli relied on any improper considera-*
> *tions in coming to his decisions.* (emphasis added)[34]

Notably, nor was there any evidence that Zaccardelli was
motivated by proper considerations. There was no evidence
because he refused to provide any. As noted, the Commission
for Public Complaints Against the RCMP has no powers to
compel testimony. In normal legal proceedings, there is a
presumption against a witness who refuses to give evidence.
In this case, Kennedy does the reverse. In the absence of any
evidence from former Commissioner Zaccardelli, he gives
him the benefit of the doubt, finding that there is no evidence of "improper considerations."

Zaccardelli's refusal to give evidence to an internal
RCMP investigation about the biggest political scandal in
recent memory should have been a bombshell of its own.
In fact, there was hardly any media coverage of the report.
One exception was *Toronto Star* columnist James Travers
whose column, "Deafening Silence on RCMP Scandal" laid
bare the key questions. Describing it as a "question that
touches democracy's sustaining legitimacy," Travers wrote:

> Zaccardelli's revealing refusal to co-operate with this
> week's public complaints report can't be left unchal-
> lenged. By not clarifying what happened and why,
> Zaccardelli is further eroding public trust in a crumbling

icon while fueling speculation that the force was set-
tling old Liberal scores while making like-minded
Conservatives come-from-behind winners.

Even by Ottawa standards, those theories are
unusually toxic. They suggest Liberals, Conservatives
and NDP prefer not to draw public attention to abuses
more typical of Third World dictatorships than First
World democracies. [35]

Travers finds two theoretical motivations for Zaccardelli's
deliberate interference in the election of 2006. One is that
as a loyalist to former Prime Minister Jean Chrétien, who
appointed him in 2000, he was keen to exact revenge against
longtime rival Paul Martin. The other theory "strengthened
by Stephen Harper's post-election visit to RCMP headquarters and budget generosity, holds that the force did
what it could to elect a law-and-order government." [36]

There is no question that the RCMP interference in the
2006 election is without precedent. Paul Kennedy's report
describes how in the 1988 election, Phil Edmunston, an
NDP candidate, brought allegations to the RCMP concerning his opponent, Progressive Conservative candidate
Richard Grise. "However, the investigating officer decided
to delay execution of the search warrants, ostensibly to
avoid influencing the election." [37] The commissioner of the
day, Norman Inkster, maintained he had no knowledge of

the affair until after the election, when Grise was charged.

In the 2008 election, it appears the RCMP reverted to previous policy and delayed the investigation into former minister of foreign affairs Maxime Bernier. Pursuing the allegations of influence peddling by his former girlfriend, Julie Couillard, the RCMP delayed interviewing Bernier until November 4, 2008 – some three weeks after the election. The *Globe and Mail* reported that the RCMP had seemed reluctant to approach Bernier during the campaign for fear of affecting his re-election.[38]

Again, several theories present themselves. The most charitable is that Zaccardelli felt the RCMP had been wrong in 1988 to avoid pursuing Grise during an election and vowed not to provide favouritism to candidates in elections ever again. The 2006 Goodale debacle led to a change in policy and kid gloves treatment for Bernier in 2008. The other theory is that the RCMP consistently protects Conservatives.

As of this writing, there has been no demand, other than from the Green Party of Canada, for a full judicial investigation of how and why the RCMP threw the 2006 election to the Conservatives. It is simply unacceptable in a democracy to ignore something as large and unacceptable as police interference in an election.

A few voices can still be heard demanding answers, like this one from the Internet magazine *The Tyee:*

We fret about each incident, but ignore the pattern. The Royal Canadian Mounted Police, like J. Edgar Hoover's FBI, has flourished for over a century on great media relations. The Mounties look gorgeous on horseback; their uniforms invoke a raw, comforting masculine power of broad shoulders, jackboots, and big pistols in big holsters. . . .

It seems unlikely, therefore, that the Mounties can be reformed by appointing the right commissioner and revising a few policies. A government that seriously wanted to clean up the RCMP would have to mount a lightning coup against it. J. Edgar Hoover protected himself by maintaining detailed files on all his political masters and enemies. The Mounties doubtless have similar files on everyone now active in politics, just as they did with Levesque.[39]

The oppressive notion of a national police force capable of blackmailing any politician is totally incongruous with our sense of ourselves as a nation. That the 2006 RCMP election-tampering scandal remains unexamined is a threat to the core of our democracy.

Chapter 6

What If They Held an Election
and No One Came?

IF SOME INDICATORS of a thriving democracy are freedom from state police interference and an independent news media, certainly another index of good health is the level of participation in elections.

The report from Canada's "election physical" is not good. As we know, the number of Canadians who vote has been dropping. The 2008 election was the lowest voter turnout in history. Since the Second World War, Canadian voter turnout had been fairly consistent at about 75 percent. But the falling off in voter participation has been notable in recent years. In 1993, 70 percent of eligible voters cast their ballots in the election that defeated Kim Campbell's Progressive Conservatives. By 1997, the turnout dropped to 67 percent, and then down again in 2000 to 61 percent. The 2004 election continued to decline with a historic low of 60.9 percent.[1] There was a slight improvement in 2006, up to 64.7 percent, but that brief blip was wiped out by the dismal level of participation in 2008: 58 percent.

The phenomenon is not exclusive to Canada. The number of people bothering to go to the polls is falling in some other modern democracies as well, but the only country with as serious a drop in voter turnout is the United Kingdom. The voter turnout in the U.K. fell from 78 percent in 1992 to 59 percent in 2001, climbing marginally to 61.4 percent in 2005.[2] Voter turnout in the United States had been low for a lot longer and more persistently. Despite high expectations for record voter turnout in the McCain–Obama contest in 2008, the analysis suggests that the vote was only about 1 percent more than in 2004. In fact, only about 61 percent of eligible American voters got out to the polls. Looking at the gap between perception and reality in the 2008 U.S. election, Curtis Gans, director of the American University's Center for the Study of the American Electorate, explained that Democrats may have increased in participation, while more Republicans stayed home.

> Many people were fooled (including this student of politics although less so than many others) by this year's increase in registration (more than 10 million added to the rolls), citizens' willingness to stand for hours even in inclement weather to vote early, the likely rise in youth and African American voting, and the extensive

grassroots organizing network of the Obama campaign into believing that turnout would be substantially higher than in 2004. But we failed to realize that the registration increase was driven by Democratic and independent registration and that the long lines at the polls were mostly populated by Democrats.[3]

When one considers that Canada's recorded percentage of participation is measured as against all eligible voters, and the U.S. percentage is measured against those who have registered to vote, the actual participation rate in the U.S. is even lower than that in Canada.

Still, in Canada we have no room for complacency. The trend lines are deeply worrying. We have now dropped to the bottom of the list of citizens' participation in choosing their government – along with the U.S., Japan, and Switzerland.

Those counties with high voter turnout leave us in their dust. A survey of European nations shows the highest rate of participation is that of Denmark, at nearly 94 percent. Among Scandinavians, voter participation is above 80 percent in all countries. Belgium has 85 percent and Austria a robust 88 percent voter turnout. Greece, the birthplace of democracy, has a 90 percent voter turnout.[4]

There is a striking correlation between those countries with high voter turnout and those countries with proportional representation in their voting systems. The low-turnout nations have in common the first-past-the-post (FPTP) system for choosing representatives for parliament. In FPTP systems, whichever candidate receives the most votes within a certain voting district wins that race. The votes for other candidates simply do not count. In countries like Sweden, Norway, Germany, Belgium, and all of the other European democracies, some measure of the vote is distributed by percentage in the number of seats in Parliament – proportional representation.

Having every vote really count increases the level of citizen participation in elections. Surveys reflect a high level of dissatisfaction among Canadians with the effectiveness of their vote. Only 14 percent of those who voted in 2000 believed their vote had made "a lot" of difference to the national result, with 28 percent of those who voted saying "none." Not surprisingly, 40 percent of those who did not vote believed their vote would make no difference at all to the country.[5]

Some nations have systems of mandatory voting. Although Australia is the best known of nations requiring its citizens to cast a ballot, more than thirty-five countries around the world have some form of compulsory voting.[6] Some, such as the Netherlands, tried the system and then abandoned it. The Netherlands had required-voting rules from 1917 until 1967. Australia introduced its system in 1924. The level of enforcement varies from country to country. Costa Rica hardly enforces at all, but with high literacy levels and a strong sense of civic engagement, Costa Rican democracy is among the healthiest in the developing world. The arguments against compulsory voting have to do with its inherently antidemocratic nature. Freedom and democracy are closely linked concepts. Requiring people to exercise their rights in a free society somehow seems a contradiction in terms. Yet, in Australia, the system is strongly favoured based on experience. A former advisor to the Australian government, Greg Barnes, offered his opinion in 2004:

> Compulsory voting has proved a resounding success in Australia. It helps to keep the cost of elections down and, most important, means that political parties don't have to raise obscene sums of money to finance their campaigns.
>
> Participating in democracy is not optional in Australia. Even if you despise politicians and the polit- ical process, you have to turn out a couple of times every three or four years to vote for your state or national government. It forces even the most cynical individual to at least cast a fleeting glance at the polit- ical process.[7]

In polls, many Canadians have said they would not like a mandatory voting system. In a major survey conducted in 2000 for Elections Canada, less than 17 percent of Canadians strongly supported compulsory voting, while 37 percent were strongly opposed.[8] Still far more had no firm view.

There are other commonalities in those countries with high citizen participation in elections. These nations also rate high in "civic literacy," which can be defined as a level of knowledge of politics combined with a sense of civic duty. It is the key and most significant indicator of health in the body politic.

Research into our levels of civic literacy was undertaken by the Royal Commission on Electoral Reform and Party Financing in 1990. It was found that the majority of Canadians were unable to answer political knowledge questions correctly. This was corroborated in a 2004 survey that revealed that only 46 percent of Canadians could answer one in three questions correctly.[9]

The parliamentary crisis in the fall of 2008, set in motion when newly re-elected Prime Minister Stephen Harper lost the confidence of the House, revealed even more worryingly, a deep deficit in Canadians' understanding of their system of government. The Dominion Institute commissioned a poll that found that 51 percent of Canadians actually believe we directly elect the prime minister.[10] Mr. Harper sought to reinforce this misperception by falsely claiming that the opposition parties were attempting to overturn the results of the election when they came together to form a coalition. While some media outlets attempted to cram an introductory course in parliamentary democracy into their news broadcast, many commercial talk-radio outlets, especially those owned by the CTVglobemedia conglomerate, were quick to fan the flames of misunderstanding. The idea that Canadians elect 308 MPs and that, in theory, any one of them could be prime minister has been completely supplanted by the cult of the leader. Admittedly, this shift has taken place over many decades and is not due to the efforts of the modern Conservative Party. Nevertheless, Mr. Harper has unquestionably gone further than any prime minister in falsely describing our electoral system to advance his ambitions. The effect has been to increase the level of civic illiteracy.

Elections Canada has a mandate not only to run elections, but to promote participation in elections. To be more precise, the chief electoral officer has a responsibility to ensure that the electoral process is accessible to all. In pursuing this mandate, former Chief Electoral Officer Jean-Pierre Kingsley commissioned some public opinion surveys.

When Canadians are polled and asked why voter turnout is falling, the respondents make a number of assumptions. The conclusions are not surprising. A couple of analysts have reported that "the majority of Canadians attribute the turnout decline to negative public attitudes toward the performance of politicians and political institutions involved in federal politics."[11]

This is a simplistic response. It is far more likely that Canadians are responding to a multiplicity of factors. While it is convenient to embrace cynicism and disgust as an explanation for lower voter turnout, lack of basic information (where to vote? why to vote? which party stands for what issue?) also drives down the level of voter participation. It is something of a chicken-and-egg conundrum: Do Canadians have a low level of political knowledge because they find politics distasteful and avert their eyes, or are Canadians quick to blame politicians to cover for a lack of civic literacy born of apathy?

It is mostly likely a dose of both. Some people are so disgusted with politicians that they don't vote as a way of indicating their disapproval. I ran into this attitude more frequently than I would have imagined possible as I went door to door in the 2008 campaign. A portion of people of every age group stated a commitment to non-voting as a protest. This was a shock to me, but researchers have been tracking the anti-voting protester, who is quite different from the non-voter who simply lacks the interest and engagement even to notice an election when it is underway.

Even more worrying than the overall results showing that Canadians do not have a strong grasp of their political system, or the ability to name their MP or MHA, MPP or MLA, is the demographic profile of that civic illiteracy. Overwhelmingly, it is the young who have the poorest scores in basic political knowledge. While 46 percent of a broad sample of Canadians were able to answer only one of three questions on political knowledge, the rate for young people ages eighteen to twenty-nine was 67 percent.

A 2004 survey found that young people were alarmingly unaware. In the last days of that campaign, only 60 percent of people in their twenties polled in a Canadian election study knew that Paul Martin was leader of the Liberals. At the beginning of the 2004 campaign, only 38 percent of people in their twenties knew who Martin was. And by the end of the campaign only 47 percent of young people knew Stephen Harper was the Conservative leader.

It is true that in the U.K, Canada and the U.S., within an unacceptably low level of overall voter turnout, is a disproportionately high level of young people's failure to vote. One researcher concluded that youth are "either apathetic (at best) or alienated (at worst)" from electoral politics.[12] There have been many academic and research efforts to explain youth disengagement from traditional politics by celebrating their level of non-traditional political activity. The fact that young people are more likely to sign a petition, participate in a rally, join a boycott or deliberately purchase goods associated with a movement for social change is highlighted in many studies: "Many individuals who did not cast a ballot still acted in a political manner, even when they themselves might not have recognized they were behaving politically," reports one Canadian study of voter behaviour.[13] The suggestion that young people are somehow just as engaged but "differently" is not very satisfying, but it does suggest we should ask why some activities are more appealing to youth than politics.

One possible explanation is that the formation of clubs based on political parties is actually forbidden in nearly every high school in Canada. Canadian high schools now routinely require community service volunteerism prior to graduation. Students can choose to donate hours to local charities or environmental groups, thus boosting their recorded community activities. Sadly, for most students the habit of volunteering does not continue through the rest of their lives, dropping off sharply once they leave high school. High schools also encourage issue-based clubs. Most Canadian high schools will boast an array of NGOs on campus. Typically there will be an Amnesty International Club, a UNICEF Club, a lesbian-gay-bisexual-transexual rights group, an anti-racism club, an environmental action group (often assigned to actually do the janitorial work of sorting recycling and composting), and so on. What you will not find on school grounds is a political party youth group. While this rule stems from concerns about excessive partisanship in school, it may be time to re-examine it in light of the alarming rates of civic illiteracy in our youth.

There certainly are differences in the reasons young people don't vote. One researcher, Henry Milner, distinguishes between "political dropouts" and "political protesters."[14]

Political dropouts are young citizens so inattentive to the political world around them that they lack the minimal knowledge needed to distinguish, and thus to choose, among parties and candidates. Political dropouts are of special concern, because they constitute a growing group of young people in established democracies who, despite being better educated on average, are less attentive to, and thus less informed about, available choices than were young people in earlier generations. Political protesters do not vote either, but unlike the dropouts, they are sufficiently informed to deliberately forego traditional means of political participation – party membership and, especially, voting – and instead undertake unconventional forms of political engagement.[15]

This increasing level of civic illiteracy should be commanding far greater levels of attention and alarm. The problem is not restricted to Canada. Looking around the world, it is clear that the youth in certain modern democracies are woefully unaware of the world around them. In an international survey that asked fifty-six questions on political knowledge, levels of political awareness tracked very closely to the levels of voting. Countries with high voting rates also have high levels of political knowledge. Swedish youth led the survey, being able to answer, on average, forty questions correctly, Germany and Italy each had on average thirty-eight questions answered correctly.

And then there is the United States, whose youth came in second to last (only Mexican youth were less knowledgeable). The young Americans could answer only twenty-three questions, while Canadian youth could answer less than half of the questions correctly (27) on average, with Great Britain at twenty-eight.[16]

Academics and researchers ponder whether the problem is due to a reduced focus on political systems and issues in basic school curricula or whether is it due to some larger social change. How many people of the baby boom generation grew up with a nightly family dinner where parents discussed politics while watching the suppertime news? As we move away from time with family, as families are busy running from one event to another in increasingly hectic and over-scheduled lives, are children and young adolescents losing the essential ingredient for civic literacy through example? Is the key to lost engagement the loss of family time in which civic literacy is passed from generation to generation? Many young people with whom I have spoken believe this to be the case. Meanwhile, it is also clear that schools spend less time on civic literacy than was the case a generation ago.

Peter Russell, professor emeritus at the University of Toronto, has lamented the failure of our educational system to prepare young people for lives as effective citizens.

It is in the schools where citizenship is shaped that there is the greatest need to bolster the educational resources of our parliamentary democracy. Here, the need is not only for teachers who are knowledgeable about the workings of our parliamentary institutions, but also for teaching materials can engage and inform young Canadians in their formative school years . . . Civic education is of vital importance for sustaining parliamentary democracy. It must be attacked with urgency. Nothing less than the essential popular foundation of our parliamentary system is at stake.[17]

As society has moved to a less engaged family integration, and less conversation around the dinner table, schools have not taken up the slack. One could argue the schools should not have to do the job of parenting. But how are young citizens supposed to become excited and engaged citizens?

As exposure to political debates in family and community has diminished, so too has media content. Studies have found a particularly poor level of civic literacy for those who watch a lot of television and rely on TV for information on current events. Those who read newspapers daily, even in the current state of heavily concentrated newspaper ownership, have a much higher rate of civic literacy.[18] Here once again, the habits of young people increase the likelihood that they will not gain exposure to solid sources of political information. International surveys confirm what we know intuitively: older people read newspapers; young people rarely do. Less than half of Canadian youth read a newspaper daily while more than 80 percent of Norwegian youth do.[19]

Other researchers think the problem lies in being deluged with too much information: "In some ways, the sheer volume of information coming from the internet and television, as well as the other media, can be over-whelming when trying to find a starting point for becom-ing informed."[20] With the advent of the Internet so much information is available but much less of it is meaningful.

Youth organizations have harnessed the Internet to engage their peers. My favourite is the youth-inspired, youth-run organization Apathy is Boring.[21] Ilona Dougherty, a young environmental activist who was planning a career in dance and choreography, founded the group after becom-ing alarmed about the low levels of youth voting in the 2004 election. With not much more than a great name for the effort, she started organizing. On a shoestring, she was successful in organizing rallies and concerts and television ads for the 2006 election. Apathy is Boring is now sup-ported by foundation funding, and Ilona and others are working full-time to increase the youth vote. Most of their activities are Web-based.

Coming from another direction, former Reform Party leader Preston Manning is also working to promote democracy. He has founded and runs the Manning Centre for Building Democracy. When asked about the persistent problem of getting youth to vote, he recalled a young man in an audience who challenged him, saying he didn't vote because he didn't think the government mattered in his life. Manning told him that he hoped the government would go back to conscription and pluck him from his comfortable life and send him on a mandatory two years of public service on Baffin Island. "Then you'd find out why it mattered to vote."[22]

Manning is on to something. It is not so much that youth would benefit from an oppressive government squashing their freedoms, as from the observation that the decline in youth voting and, in fact, the decline in voting across all age groups, corresponds with an era when the dominant ideology has denigrated the role of government. While Manning chose to identify the threat of a more activist government, his fanciful suggestion did alert me to another question: how do youth see the role of government in their lives? I am afraid they think government is irrelevant.

The 1990s saw a triumphalist, neo-conservative celebration of the "private sector," with an attendant demonization of Big Government. The Lockeian and Jeffersonian notions of liberal democracy were crushed. The new framing of issues was designed to accelerate a political agenda of globalization and corporate rule. It sought to cut regulations, taxes, and public services. "Getting government out of our faces" was a rallying cry of the Mike Harris government in Ontario, echoing the Thatcher and Reagan chorus of the 1980s. Deregulation, privatization, and trade liberalization went hand in hand with calls to cut taxes and government spending. "Government" shifted from being a servant of democracy to being an unwanted intrusion.

It is little wonder that so many young people who have never lived through an era when government was a partner, a friend, and the embodiment of the democratic aspirations of the body politic would not see the point in engaging in government processes.

My father, now in his eighties and living in Cape Breton, grew up in London during the Blitz. His youth was dominated by war. First he worked in the Home Guard, building air raid shelters, helping the elderly increase the safety of their homes, taping over windows to reduce the chances of shattering glass injuring them as bombs dropped nearby. He experienced the loss of friends and neighbours to the air strikes in his own neighbourhood before being old enough to join the army. When I was a child, my mother explained why our daddy couldn't come to fireworks celebrations with us like other children's fathers. The shell bursts would cause him to break out in a cold sweat.

So, I was taken aback when he recently observed, "You know, I really preferred the Second World War." When I expressed disbelief, he explained, "Well, you see, then you really felt the government was on your side."

The ideology of the neo-conservative right of "government as enemy" has ended up decreasing voter turnout. A return to "government as friend" may be in our future in response to the economic downturn; President Barack Obama may yet be a new FDR with a Green New Deal. But for now, the disturbing elements described thus far, from the centralization of power in the PMO, to the concentration of media in a handful of owners who largely, if not entirely, adhere to the doctrine of "government as enemy," all contribute to conditions that lower the likelihood of high voter turnout.

In addition, the 2008 election had the additional deterrent of a new Elections Law. The law was brought into being in response to a non-problem — the risk of voter fraud. It exacerbated a real crisis.

Recently appointed Chief Electoral Officer Marc Mayrand was asked to rule on the question of accepting women in traditional Islamic dress, with faces covered, to vote. Based on the existing law, he ruled that people whose faces were not visible could vote, if they swore an oath and had witnesses who were prepared to vouch for their identity, or if they were willing to unveil privately, in circumstances consistent with their religious practices. In the House of Commons, Prime Minister Stephen Harper went on the attack against Mayrand. There was no love lost between the Conservative Party and Elections Canada. In a spat over what candidates could legally say in ads, Stephen Harper attacked Jean-Pierre Kingsley back in 2002, "This is the kind of garbage we're getting into — and more shockingly the kind of garbage that Jean-Pierre Kingsley and people at Elections Canada increasingly think is their business."[23]

The departure of Kingsley was linked to the hostility between his office and the Harper government. Kingsley had angered the Conservative Party when he ruled that the fees for their convention should properly be declared as donations and reported as such. When Kingsley retired, media observers speculated that the relationship with the Harper government had been the determining factor in his decision.[24] Now Marc Mayrand was receiving tongue lashings in Question Period from a prime minister who sensed a way to appeal to the least attractive part of his base. By suggesting that Elections Canada was asleep at the switch on election fraud, or even a dormant domestic terrorist threat, Harper appealed to both anti-government and xenophobic elements at the same time. An earlier dispute over voting had led to a series of recommendations to tighten up voter eligibility. There had been an accusation of voter fraud in Toronto Centre in the 2000 election and although it was established that nothing untoward had occurred in that riding, a House Committee took on the challenge of proposing better voting rules. Their work gave the Harper government elements of what they wanted — a legislative attempt to address the non-issue of voter fraud by veiled Islamic women.

The result in the 2008 election was disastrous. The new rules required that voters were allowed to cast a ballot only if they had a valid government-issued photo ID as well as proof of their current address. There were allowances for people without those forms of identification to vote if they were accompanied to the polling station by someone who had those proofs and who came for the purpose of serving as a witness. On top of the problem of new rules, the Elections Canada returning officers received inadequate and inconsistent training. The fact that the prime minister had called four by-elections within the month before asking for a new election in early September 2008 may have stretched Elections Canada's resources. Each of the four by-elections required the establishment of $3 million worth of operations. The snap election call for October 14, which broke the new fixed election date law, may not have caught only opposition parties by surprise. It seems also to have caught Elections Canada unprepared.

Based on anecdotal reports, I estimate conservatively that tens of thousands of Canadians who went to their polling station on October 14 intending to vote were turned away. One survey at St. Francis Xavier University in Antigonish, Nova Scotia, found that 30 percent of the students who attempted to vote were denied.[25]

For those Canadians who assume that everyone carries a valid driver's licence with a current address, the new rules seemed very reasonable. But in a real way we are slipping backward to the days when only those who owned property could vote. Low-income Canadians are unlikely to have a driver's licence or any other type of valid government-issued photo ID. Rural Canadians often have a driver's licence that includes a post box address. This will not satisfy the new law. Students and other young people may lack a driver's licence and many move frequently, making them unable to provide adequate proof of residence. Older Canadians have let their driver's licences lapse and lack other valid ID. Aboriginal Canadians also tend to lack the required ID. Even some of the well-heeled were caught off guard. Some people who brought a passport to the polling station found that it was not adequate since it does not include an address.

One horrified returning officer with decades of experience wrote of the debacle in the Halifax *Chronicle-Herald*. He recounted having to turn away his own relatives because they had not brought a witness with them! In Vancouver, Green Party volunteers watched as outraged seniors ripped up their voting cards when told they were not allowed to vote despite having voted at the same address for decades. In Halifax, students were reported to have been turned away "in droves." One Pictou County, Nova Scotia resident told me how "humiliating" it was to be denied the right to vote even though everyone in his rural polling station knew him. Elections Canada training had convinced returning officers that a voter had to bring a witness for the specific purpose of attesting to his or her identity, and that an accidental witness would not do.

The lowest voter turnout in Canadian history may have had more to do with the new voting rules than anyone has yet determined. The Green Party lodged a complaint with Elections Canada, but the other parties have stayed silent. Perhaps they feel hindered by the fact that they voted for the legislation. Undoubtedly, the bad experience for voters who were turned away will carry over to the next election and continue to depress voter turnout. The only way to reverse this trend is through a high-profile repeal or significant amendment of the new law.

The October 14, 2008 election occurred when many Canadians were distracted by the dramatic and historic presidential race south of the border. The English-language Canadian leaders' debate certainly lost viewers to the U.S. vice-presidential debate between Sarah Palin and Joseph Biden. It also lost voters by the fact that it was the briefest election campaign in Canadian history, with Election Day being the Tuesday after the three-day Thanksgiving holiday weekend. Low voter turnout clearly aided the governing party.

In his post-election analysis, Stephen Maher, the Ottawa correspondent for the *Chronicle-Herald,* nailed the issue:

Prime Minister Stephen Harper told reporters that it was too bad that only 59.1 percent of Canadians bothered to vote Tuesday.

"We're obviously disappointed by voter turnout," he said. "It's low and been getting lower for some time now."

Mr. Harper is not at all disappointed that more people didn't vote in this election, since he has been working diligently for almost two years to make sure that the Liberals stayed home.

On Tuesday, 13,832,972 Canadians marked an X — a million fewer than in 2006.

Every party except the Greens lost votes, but the Liberals were the big losers — 854,425 votes.

Mr. Harper didn't win by persuading Liberals to vote Tory. He won by persuading Liberals to stay home.[26]

If we yearn for the quickening of democracy, for young and old to flock to the polls, for people to engage in well-informed civic discourse and to vote in large numbers, we need to create an atmosphere that encourages participation. Creating a culture imbued with a sense of civic duty is not a naïve or quixotic goal.

Chapter 7

Follow the Money

THE MIXTURE OF MONEY AND POLITICS can be an unsavoury combination. The influence of foreign money in displacing Progressive Conservative Leader Joe Clark, recounted earlier, is just one example. Money is the grease in the political machine. Money means influence and power. Money dictates winners and losers.

The Watergate-era adage "Follow the money" takes a political observer to topics like the role of lobbyists, the funding of political campaigns, and the retirement packages of political leaders. It does seem to be the case that many people leave politics wealthier than when they entered. Yet the salaries of public officials are never close to those of people who are successful in the corporate world. There is some fiscal alchemy along the way. Some people seem to turn leaden public careers into personal gold.

It was not long ago that Ottawa was a capital city with very few lobbyists. It is a change that veteran MPs often comment on. Both the late Jim Fulton, who served as an NDP MP from 1979 to 1993, and Progressive Conservative MP and former Speaker John Fraser, who served from 1972 to 1993, have expressed to me their dismay at the rise in professional lobbying firms in Ottawa.[1] Until the 1980s, professional lobbying firms simply did not exist in Canada. But by 2008, the number of registered lobbyists had doubled over the 1989 level, the first year in which lobbyists were required to register.[2]

And now, politicians speak of lobbying as though it were an important part of the fabric of democracy. In an open letter accompanying changes to the *Lobbyist Registration Act* in early 2008, Minister of Justice Vic Toews wrote that "lobbying is a legitimate and necessary part of our democratic system."[3]

Lobbying politicians may well be an *accepted* part of our democracy, but to describe it as "necessary" stretches the point. Endorsing the role of professional lobby firms (which now prefer to go under the more benign label of "government relations" firms) implies acceptance of the notion that those with money and insider knowledge are entitled to superior access to government and policy decisions. The growth in professional lobbyists is essentially antidemocratic.

Companies such as Hill & Knowlton, Government Consultants International (GCI), Earnscliffe Strategy Group,

Temple Scott Associates, and others troll the halls of government. A retainer for a lobby firm is routinely $3,000–$10,000 a month, with hourly rates of $150–$500.[4] If a citizen truly needs the intermediation of a lobbyist to get the attention of policy-makers in Ottawa, as Vic Toews's letter suggests, then we have no real democracy.

Lobbyists run any number of efforts, from simply mapping the bureaucracy to assist clients make their own way to the right door (this is the story they emphasize repeatedly for public consumption), to obtaining access to politicians, to running campaigns to distort the truth in media.

One good example of the latter is recorded on the Non-Smokers' Rights Association website. The group details how tobacco-industry front groups are set up under the watchful tutelage of lobbying firms. Specifically, GCI is referenced for its assistance to R.J. Reynolds Tobacco in putting forward a front group called the "Smokers' Freedom Society."[5] The tobacco company was behind the scenes, footing the bill for what was intended to look like a spontaneous public expression for support for the right to smoke. The tar sands companies are using similar strategies to try to clean up their image.

The death by Taser of Robert Dziekanski at the Vancouver Airport led Arizona-based Taser International to turn to a Canadian consultant for help. With an RCMP investigation underway, Taser hired Hill & Knowlton's

Canadian operations. The choice of consultant by the Taser corporation is revealing. Dziekanski had been killed October 14. On November 28, 2007, Hill & Knowlton lobbyist Ken Boessenkool registered as a lobbyist for Taser. Boessenkool had worked closely with Stephen Harper during the 2004 and 2006 elections.[6]

That pattern repeats itself over and over again, despite the fact that longer cooling-off periods are continually recommended for people leaving political work and entering the private sector. Prime Minister Harper's first chief of staff, Ian Brodie, who served with him at the Canadian Alliance Party then in the PMO, resigned on July 1, 2008. Within six months he had landed at Hill & Knowlton as senior Ottawa counsel. To avoid violating the "cooling-off" period rules, he is not supposed to lobby while advising the lobby firm on policy.[7] While in opposition Stephen Harper had railed against the revolving door of influence-trading and lobbyists, promising to bring in strict reforms to the lobbying system, but nothing has yet been forthcoming.

The process of registering lobbyists began under the Mulroney government in 1989. The *Lobbyists Registration Act* essentially puts the onus on lobbyists to register, pay a fee, and list their areas of interest. By its very principles, the Act legitimizes the role of the lobbying industry.

Four basic principles are set out in the preamble to the Act:

1. Free and open access to government is an important matter of public interest.

2. Lobbying public office holders is a legitimate activity.

3. It is desirable that public office holders and the general public be able to know who is attempting to influence government.

4. The system for the registration of paid lobbyists should not impede free and open access to government.

There are many loopholes. Democracy Watch, the leading citizen watchdog on the need to tighten controls on lobbyists, has consistently called for tougher and better rules. In the 2006 election campaign, Democracy Watch had praised the Conservative Party for its platform pledge to bring in a new law to "require ministers and senior government officials to record their contacts with lobbyists." This has not been done. The law that was brought in by the Harper government requires only that "arranged meetings" and oral communications be reported, and then only if these are initiated by the lobbyist. Email messages and letters are not covered by the Act.

Whereas now someone like Ian Brodie can move from the top political appointment in the country, chief of staff to the prime minister, to serving as advisor to a major lobbying firm attempting to influence that same prime minister within six months, Democracy Watch argues the cooling-off period should be five years.

As it now stands, lobbyists can be in contact with public office holders and no one needs to report that contact. In a December 2008 release, Democracy Watch Coordinator Duff Conacher, in referring to the Mulroney–Schreiber scandal, made it clear why Canada's rating on the UN Corruption Index has continued to worsen:

> The federal government's accountability enforcement system is the scandal because, among many other highly questionable activities, it is still effectively legal for a person like Karlheinz Schreiber to fundraise for and make secret donations to nomination race and party leadership candidates, to lobby in secret, to make secret, fixed deals with Cabinet ministers, their staff, hand-picked Cabinet patronage appointees and government employees, and for everyone involved to be dishonest about their secret, unethical relationships . . .
>
> Incredibly, it is much more likely Canadians will be caught and punished for parking illegally than a politician will be caught and punished taking money from a lobbyist.[8]

The other worrying feature of the world of lobbying is that, as with the media, there has been an aggressive buying out of small firms by larger ones. The concentration of ownership means that the Canadian lobby groups are all now branch plants of global enterprises. Two companies alone, both founded in the 1980s, WPP and Omnicon, control 80 percent of the world's lobbying, public relations, and advertising firms. Does it matter? The U.S. non-profit group Center for Media and Democracy has identified concerns. Journalists Sharon Beder and Richard Gosden have dubbed WPP "World Propaganda Power," although the firm's name comes from Wire and Plastic Products, a small U.K. company that morphed into a lobbying giant. Publishing in the Center for Media and Democracy newsletter *PRWatch.org,* Beder and Gosden describe the power of such firms in "selling" war. Their focus was on WPP, which, in a hostile takeover of the J. Walter Thompson Group, got Hill & Knowlton in the bargain.

> Does it matter that four of the world's largest public relations firms are now owned by the same corporation? WPP is a potential powerhouse, a huge propaganda machine, with the reach and coordinated skills in people manipulation that might allow it to rule the hearts and minds of the entire global population.
>
> Some ad men and PR flacks have long dreamed of such a tool. Even back in the early 1980's, when J. Walter Thomson was small fry compared to its WPP parent today, one of its executives went on record musing, 'We have within our hands the greatest

aggregate means of mass education and persuasion the world has ever seen – namely, the channels of advertising communication. We have power. Why do we not use it?' WPP is a UK-based company. This means that when Hill & Knowlton masterminded the Kuwaiti campaign to sell the Gulf War to the American public, the owners of this highly effective propaganda machine were residing in another country. Should this give pause for thought? Does it demonstrate a certain potential for the future exercise of global political power? The power to manipulate democratic political processes through managing public opinion, which Hill & Knowlton demonstrated 10 years ago, is trifling compared to the potential power now residing in integrated conglomerates like WPP and Omnicom.[9]

In examining the lower public respect for politicians and the level of scandal and corruption within government, one sees a clear relationship to the number of lobbyists at work in Ottawa. This may not be cause and effect. It may simply be symptomatic of the corrupted value system of our entire society.

Professor Kenneth Melchin, theologian and ethicist at St. Paul's University in Ottawa, explains our deteriorating moral condition as due to the adoption, holus-bolus, of market theory into everyday life.[10] Our society has taken this theory of economics that assumes that everyone will make an economically rational decision and applied it to moral decision making – with disastrous results. Ergo, it is thought that everyone always acts to improve their bottom line. In other words, all citizens are exclusively self-interested. This may be fine for market-based economic theory, but it is surely disastrous for human affairs. All of us are somewhat self-interested and also somewhat altruistic. In a healthy society and functioning democracy, one must hope that altruism comes to the fore a great deal more often than naked self-interest.

Political parties have pitched their campaign promises to a public assumed to be entirely self-interested. These assumptions tend to have a self-fulfilling nature. When the Canadian public expressed strong support in polls for placing taxes on pollution and reducing taxes on income, the Conservative and NDP messaging to oppose these measures during the 2008 election campaign was a direct appeal to fear and self-interest. Instead of promoting the measure as sound economic and environmental policy, which was the view of nearly every expert in both fields, the parties opposing carbon taxes raised fears that gas prices would go up and other taxes would not be reduced. An appeal to the public good would not have been in line with their view of dominant values.

Sadly, our society is so contaminated with the notion that acting for greed and self-interest is "normal" that we have weakened the essential fibre of society. Cheating has become epidemic. Leading accounting firms have cooked the books. Enron took a number down with them in their unethical attempt to defraud their shareholders, employees, and society as a whole. Even scientists and academics fudge their research to get better grants. In the 2008 leaders' debate, the rules were clear. No crib notes or background papers were allowed. We were all told that blank index cards would be available for note taking. Stephen Harper's staff took care to print out background notes on index cards, but they picked the wrong-sized cards. And no one writes in printer font. Looking over from my seat, I remember the shock of realizing he was cheating. I felt as though I was back in grade school. Do you "tattle" on a cheater? Now, all I can think is "What were his staff thinking?" It is clear they thought he wouldn't be caught.

The values that were once accepted as the mark of a decent citizen – "My word is my bond," or "I have nothing but my good name" – seem laughably outdated. We live in a society whose essential values have been transactionalized. Economic rationality operates without shame to find the best deal. In such a value scheme, the only limit on avaricious behaviour is the risk of getting caught. Thus, the word *ethics* is increasingly employed not to describe how we live together in fairness, cooperation, and love, but has shifted to mean a prescribed set of rules to constrain the "natural" tendency of all humans, including public office holders, to cash in. *Ethics* as a word meaning behaviour habituated to virtue has been replaced by a set of reporting requirements and red tape.

Corruption in government is hardly new. From the Teapot Dome to Airbus, scandals and rumours of scandals have rocked politics. But the shift in social values has resulted in a troubling decline in virtue. This downward spiral has its new poster child every few months. Former Illinois Governor Rod Blagojevich may have hit a new low when he was alleged in December 2008 to have trolled for the biggest bribe to fill President Barack Obama's vacant Illinois Senate seat. Then along came "well-respected Wall Street investor" Bernard Madoff and allegations that he pulled off a $50-billion scheme to defraud those who placed their trust in him. Cheaters abound and lawmakers are simply not keeping up.

Democracy Watch has taken the Harper government to court on its broken fixed election date law and broken promises on lobbying laws. It might be easy to dismiss the criticisms from this valiant NGO, assuming it would never be satisfied with government action, except that Duff Conacher was so pleased with the Conservative Party platform in 2006. When I was working for Sierra Club of Canada, terrified of Stephen Harper's climate policies and how he would demolish the limited progress we were finally making, Duff and I used to argue about Stephen Harper. He was completely impressed with the Conservative platform on government accountability. The *Federal Accountability Act* failed to live up to its promise. In fact, one unexpected element of it was to remove the "duty to act honestly" from senior government officials and members of Cabinet.

Democracy Watch and other public reformers are not without their successes. Until very recently large corporations could make massive political donations. Democracy Watch tracked the level of corporate donations in 2002 and determined empirically what was obvious intuitively: corporations gave larger donations to the governing party: "The study reveals a clear pattern of large donations to the Liberals, and significant lobbying efforts, by most of the corporations that receive the most federal government contract dollars," said Democracy Watch board member Aaron Freeman.[11]

Regulating and controlling political donations has been on the agenda of successive governments for decades. This is one area where huge progress has been made. The first legislative effort was in 1974 when the government of Pierre Trudeau brought in the country's first electoral financing law. It set out spending limits, reporting requirements, allowable income tax donations for support to political parties and campaigns and systems for public reimbursement of candidate expenses. The goal of the reform was clear: big money should not call the shots in Canadian elections. As the 1974 bill was under debate, the leader of the New Democratic Party, David Lewis, supported the reforms. "Elections," he said, "ought not to be the property of those who can get the largest amount of money . . . at election time."[12]

The 1974 rules brought some limits to the system, but also left many large holes. No one was required to publish the list of who donated to nomination or leadership races. Large corporate and trade union donations were legal and had an impact on political parties and on the governments they formed. Improving the fairness of electoral financing was well canvassed in the 1991 Royal Commission on Electoral Reform and Party Financing (Lortie Commission). Public interest groups and reports from chief electoral officers identified areas that required improvement. The pressure for better controls led to a 2002 promise from Prime Minister Jean Chrétien to tackle election financing again.

The reforms he ushered in were substantial and went a long way toward eliminating the power of money in election financing. Donations from corporations and labour unions were eliminated. Only donations from individuals resident in Canada or Canadian citizens abroad are allowed. The donation limit was set at $10,000, but has since been reduced under Prime Minister Harper to $1,100 to a federal party and a total of $1,100 to riding associations (now called "electoral district associations" or EDAs). The Act called for the creation of legally registered electoral district associations in order to allow those party entities to receive funds properly. At the same time, the tax benefits for political party donations were improved, allowing a 75 percent refund for donations up to $400. The rules in Canada make it far easier for someone of modest means without well-heeled donors to become elected.

The reform package also required full reporting of the donor list for internal party contests for leadership and placed spending limits on leadership campaigns. The new rules would have made it illegal for Stephen Harper to keep secret the names of his supporters when he sought the Alliance Party leadership. It is a shame that the list of his donors has never been released.

As well as regulating how political parties raise their money, the Act regulates how the money is spent. The amount allowed to be spent during a campaign, called the "writ period," is controlled. For the 2006 election, for example, no party was allowed to spend more than $18.3 million on advertising. That amount will seem more than adequate to Canadians at the receiving end of the advertising. However, the Conservatives found the $18.3 million cap restrictive and sought ways to evade the limits. Each EDA also had spending limits of $80,000 and many would not be spending the full amount. Conservative Party senior organizers decided this created an opportunity.

If EDAs with "space" to spend could be sent money which was then redirected back to Conservative headquarters for advertising, they figured the cost of national advertising could be augmented with the money funnelled back from the underspending ridings. The added benefit was that in spending the full $80,000, each EDA would receive a refund of 60 percent of what was spent. It seemed like a win-win plan. Foolproof. So sixty-seven campaigns that were not likely to win and not going to spend the full amount were asked to accept money from Conservative HQ and then send it back. Elections Canada did not think this was "win-win." In fact, they told all sixty-seven EDAs that the campaign spending had violated the *Elections Act*. This became known as the "In-Out Scandal."

I heard about it in detail from a former 2006 Conservative candidate who decided to run for the Green Party in 2008. In 2006 Gary Caldwell had run in the Eastern Townships riding of Compton–Stanstead for the Conservative Party. Conservative HQ had asked him to accept a cheque and send the amount right back for use in Quebec advertising. He was told it was legal and he agreed. When Elections Canada contacted him after the election, he was asked about his financial report and questioned whether or not the money received was actually spent in his riding. When he explained that it had not been, he was told he had violated the *Elections Act*. He apologized, asked to refile his financial report, and paid back some amount of money. Gary Caldwell is a fine and decent person. He felt badly that his party had misled him, but he wasn't furious until he discovered that he was named as a co-plaintiff with the Conservative Party of Canada in a suit against Elections

Canada. Unlike Gary Caldwell, when the Conservative Party was told by Elections Canada that it had overspent on advertising by approximately $1 million, it decided to sue the federal overseer of fair elections. No one from the party had contacted Caldwell before using his name in litigation. In court documents it was claimed that he objected to Elections Canada's opinion, which is precisely what he had not done.

Reflecting on his disenchantment with the Conservatives, Caldwell told CTV News, "Parliament, of course, was a deliberative forum. It was a place where people who were representatives of the electors engaged in a public debate . . . There have been a lot of things that contribute to that changing, and now we have cynical power machines who . . . have reduced candidates and members of Parliament to the role of puppets. It's a real issue, a real concern, and it can only be changed by grass-roots parties."[13]

Gary Caldwell wasn't the only candidate who was outraged. Two Conservative candidates in Newfoundland and Labrador had no idea they too were involved in the scandal until the media called them in connection with the RCMP search warrants on Conservative Party headquarters in April 2008. Joe Goudie, a former provincial Cabinet minister, was blunt in his assessment of the Harper Conservatives. "I'm completely upset that the Conservative Party of Canada and its leader used me this way for their own ends, whatever those ends are proven to be," he told CBC News.[14]

The lawsuit has had the effect of delaying the day of reckoning on the 2006 campaign overspending by the Conservatives. Election spending laws are critical, as is enforcing them, but they are complicated and somewhat bureaucratic. It remains to be seen where the election law violations, if proven, will end up on the political Richter scale.

The funding of political parties is a critical part of democracy. The Lortie Commission made it clear that democracy means more than a chance to mark an X every few years. It means the opportunity to be fully informed before you mark that X. As the report of that commission explained, "Elections are fair and equitable only if all citizens are reasonably informed of all the possible choices and if parties and candidates are given a reasonable opportunity to present their positions."[15]

The ability to inform citizens has been interpreted as having the ability to run advertising and to run campaigns – and that means money. The funding of political parties from public sources is a major reform in our democracy, and is the case in many countries around the world. Even the United States offers some public financing for election campaigns.

The 2003 election financing reforms could only remove the ability to raise funds from corporations and labour unions by finding another source of support to replace those sources. It is speculated around Ottawa that the government of the day had legal advice that it would be constitutionally unsound to abolish donations from corporations and unions unless a public subsidy was provided. That public subsidy took the form of a small amount per vote.

As Chief Electoral Officer Jean-Pierre Kingsley explained at the time, "Each party's quarterly allowance will be 37.5 cents times the total number of valid votes that party received in the previous general election (which equates to $1.50 per vote, when calculated over a full year). The quarterly allowance is viewed as *offsetting forgone revenues as a result of the proposed ban or restrictions on corporate and trade union contributions*" (emphasis added).[16]

It was $1.50 initially and has increased over time. The small amount per vote is often cited by Green Party supporters as a reason they feel good about voting for the party, even when they are certain we cannot win a seat in their riding. It goes some way toward rebalancing the unfairness of the First Past the Post system, which creates large hurdles for emerging national parties. It is harder to win seats in FPTP but at least each vote counts for something. For the larger, more established parties, public financing reduces the unsavoury influence of donors who hope to use those donations as down payments on future political favours. Public financing both reduces the clout of deep pockets in Canadian elections and provides a more egalitarian system for all parties in our multiparty system.

Stephen Harper's attempt to slash the public subsidy to

political parties in the fall 2008 economic statement was crass political opportunism of the worst kind. Instead of a package of necessary stimuli to help Canada kick-start its economy as it slid into recession, Harper's government took aim at its political adversaries. The reaction was incendiary, with all opposition parties united in a determination to vote "no confidence" and take a coalition government option to the governor general.

A full debate on the merits of public financing never happened. Minister of Finance Jim Flaherty removed the threat to eliminate public financing of political parties within days. The retreat left the Canadian public with a sense of having been sideswiped by a rapidly moving vehicle. Some Canadians were left wondering why the government would have chosen to try to kill such an important aspect of democratic and fair elections. Others learned for the first time that political parties were getting tax support, and they didn't like it. Without an explanation that this small funding was established in order to eliminate other kinds of donations, why would any taxpayer like the idea of public support to political parties? Eighty percent of Canadians have said they would never want to join a party.[17] Why would they want to be taxed to support a club they do not want to join?

In fiscal terms, the total cost of the political party per vote subsidy is tiny. The *total* amount to the Conservatives, Liberals, Bloc Québécois, New Democrats, and Green

Party is only $26 million. That sounds like a lot of money, especially when linked to the question "Why should the taxpayer be supporting these political parties?" Phrased in such terms, in the wake of Harper's disastrous economic statement, online poll after online poll found low levels of public support for this subsidy. When placed in context, that $26 million is about 0.01 percent of the total spending within the $250 billion federal budget. Killing that support had absolutely nothing to do with fiscal prudence or facing an economic crisis. It had absolutely everything to do with partisan advantage. It was about trying to actually bankrupt the Liberal Party. That it would deliver a body blow to all the other opposition parties was just collateral damage.

A friend of mine who once worked in Harper's inner circle asked him, "What will you do about the Liberal Party?" He recounts that Harper didn't take a moment to reply, "I am going to bankrupt them." This much-desired goal of the Harper team became public through a book by Harper's mentor and friend Tom Flanagan. As former Liberal Party director Jamie Carroll put it, "Tom Flanagan – a very bright man who has been the eminence grise of the Conservative movement in Canada for almost two decades – made the jaw-dropping assertion some months ago that the long-term mission of the Conservative Party was to destroy the Liberal Party of Canada; to ensure they are 'pushed into a financial pit they can never climb out of.'"[18]

As often is the case when Stephen Harper is hell-bent

on power, he does not pause to consider the public policy damage occasioned by his ambition. In this case, the cloud over public financing of political parties will remain unless and until its underlying rationale is adequately explained. Harper's timing was exquisite. Had he suggested in the spring 2008 session of Parliament that the funding for parties was under reconsideration, it is unlikely that political parties would have borrowed money. All the parties were counting on that payment as a security for loans to run their campaigns. I know that the Green Party would not have taken out loans based on our anticipated repayment based on the per vote subsidy if we had any doubt the system would remain in place.

The Conservative Party, to its credit, has built up a very effective fundraising base. Of course, each donation receives a tax benefit – another form of public subsidy. It would be able to withstand losing the per vote subsidy, and would emerge stronger as the other parties faced the prospect of bankruptcy.

Moving to remove the per vote public financing would be a first step to reversing the progress in electoral reform. The courts might well rule that it was not constitutional to remove the public subsidy without allowing fundraising from other sources. In no time the prohibitions against accepting corporate and union money would be reversed and we would return to the bad old days of Canadian election financing.

At a time when we should be concentrating on following the money and moving forward with better controls on lobbyists, tighter prohibitions against unreported money, and ensuring that foreign money cannot be used to depose a political party leader, ironically the country's largest debate is over the one area where we have accomplished meaningful reform. We need to keep the per vote subsidy, but it alone cannot ensure a functioning, healthy democracy. In fact, on the evidence, we know it does not.

Chapter 8

Making the Vote Fair

As we diagnose the ills of the body politic in Canada, it is urgent that solutions be identified. We are moving in a dangerous direction in which fewer people vote, less relevant information is available to the voter, and power is increasingly concentrated in the hands of the prime minister. Reforming political financing has made much progress, but true transparency and accountability are still elusive. Other more meaningful reforms are clearly necessary.

When Canadian political and media attention turns to the question of reforming the way parliamentarians are chosen, the focus is nearly always on the Senate. Abolish it? Elect it? Or, more recently, stack it?

The problem is that changing the way senators are selected will have little impact on voter turnout in general elections. While an elected Senate may sound like a great leap forward for democracy, it is unlikely to address any of the concerns identified in this book. It will not make the way we elect a government fairer. Far from arresting the trend toward the Americanization of our political system, it will hasten it.

The U.S. system has checks and balances in a House and Senate that thwart each other and that collectively thwart the executive in the big white house at 1600 Pennsylvania Avenue. Parliamentary democracy does not contain these checks and balances. We do not elect a prime minister. We elect 308 members of Parliament and, in theory, they choose the prime minister. There is no real division between executive and legislative. While the Senate has the power to thwart the will of the House, it is constrained not being elected. Sober second thought is kept very sober by virtue of being unelected and lacking the legitimacy to routinely obstruct the will of the House – and by extension, that of the Canadian people. The clamour to have an elected Senate may have a long hangover if our Parliament begins to suffer U.S.-style gridlock.

On the other hand, reforming the way we elect members of Parliament could address a number of the worrying elements of our democratic decline. Research shows that those countries with proportional representation have much higher voter turnout than countries with first-past-the-post (FPTP) – or single member plurality (SMP) – voting systems. Proportional representation countries tend to have higher levels of civic literacy. They also have a larger number of women and minority ethnic groups elected to their national parliaments.

These salutary effects of proportional representation are actually only incidental benefits from the main advantage: getting the government we vote for.

Under the FPTP system, we run the gravest risk to a democratic nation: a false majority.

The term *false majority* was coined by University of Toronto political scientist Peter Russell, now professor emeritus. A false majority occurs when a where the majority of parliamentary seats are won by a party that received a minority of popular support. Russell's most recent book, *Two Cheers for Minority Government,* is important reading for any Canadian concerned for our nation's future.[1] Russell concentrates on how to make minority governments work, but clearly views the risk of a false majority as a far greater threat to democracy than a series of minorities, as we are now experiencing.

When one considers the accumulation of power in the hands of the Canadian prime minister, one can see that the balancing and concomitant powers of the House, opposition parties, government backbenchers, even Cabinet members and the civil service are essential to rebalance the exercise of that power. In a situation of a false majority government, the prime minister can pursue an agenda contrary to the wishes of the majority of the public, and no institution in our system can serve as a counterweight — that is until the next election. With a false majority, that electoral chance may not come around again for years. With a minority, there are, at least, some constraints. As constitutional expert Eugene Forsey once observed, "A government without a clear majority is more likely to stop, look and listen."[2]

Of course, Eugene Forsey passed away before encountering the minority government of Stephen Harper.

A false majority represents a clear threat to democracy, yet it is entirely legitimate within our electoral system. While the next chapter examines ways to live with minority parliaments, this chapter explores ways to fix our electoral system so that we have a Parliament that actually reflects the way Canadians voted. This is the single most effective antidote to what ails our political system.

The FPTP system hails from the eleventh century. Yes, it's true. We have a voting system invented when people thought the earth was flat. It has survived through history in times with no political parties and through the era when two parties prevailed. In such times, the flaws in the system were tolerable. People voted either Tory or Grit and, generally speaking, the party that won the most seats represented the voters' preferences. This is demonstrably no longer the case.

Unlike the United States, Canada has had a multiparty system since the 1920s. There were third-party entities between 1867 and the Roaring Twenties, but they did not run full slates. Still, even before 1920, smaller parties occasionally had an impact on the election results. For example, in the 1896 election a farmers' party called "Patrons of Industry" ran in twenty-six ridings and a splinter Conservative party group opposed to French-language education ran in nine ridings. The two small parties managed to gain 9 percent of the popular vote between them and succeeded in keeping the Liberals under Prime Minister Wilfrid Laurier in government with the majority of seats, but with 1 percent less of the popular vote than the Conservatives. The 1896 election resulted in the first evidence of the biggest risk to democracy due to the FPTP system — a false majority.

Since the 1920s and the advent of a multiple parties on the Canadian political landscape, minority parliaments and false majorities have become far more common. The smaller parties have come and gone — Labour, Unionist, Progressive — but even Mackenzie King was held to a minority government due to the multiparty system.

Between 1867 and 1920, Canada never experienced a minority government. Since 1920, we have had thirteen. Even more troubling, we have had *twelve* false majority governments. These are majority governments formed even when the majority of the voters voted for a party other than the one that gained the largest seat count. This is only possible due to the FPTP system.

The last *true majority* government, where the ruling party won *both* the majority of seats and the majority of the popular vote, was in 1984. Brian Mulroney was reported to

have won by a landslide. In truth, his party's 211 seats —
representing 75 percent of the House — represented a bare
sliver above 50 percent of the popular vote. Nevertheless,
that is a lot closer to majority public support than the
"majorities" enjoyed by Jean Chrétien in 1993, who won 177
seats with 41 percent of the vote, dropping to another
"majority" with 39 percent of the vote in 1997. Mulroney
also enjoyed a false majority in his last mandate, winning 43
percent of the popular vote and the majority of seats.

The historic assumption of Canadian politics, that false
majorities and minority governments are exceptions to
the rule, is no longer true. In fact, as long as we are in a
multiparty system, the most likely results in elections will
be either minority governments or false majorities.

Meanwhile the FPTP system increases voter dissatisfaction by leaving millions of Canadians "orphaned" by the
voting system. The non-government group, Fair Vote
Canada, tracks orphan voters, the voters whose votes fail
to register anywhere except for the per vote subsidy. In the
2008 election, Fair Vote Canada estimated the number of
orphan voters at 7 million – or just slightly above 50 percent
of the valid votes cast. That includes, of course, the historic
high-water mark of a party winning a large popular vote
without electing MPs, the nearly 1 million votes for the
Green Party. It also includes Conservative voters in
downtown Toronto, Liberal voters in Alberta, and New
Democratic Party voters everywhere. The NDP actually got

1 million votes more than the Bloc Québécois, yet won far fewer seats. The Bloc won 50 seats with 1.3 million votes, while the NDP won 37 seats with 2.4 million votes. The Green Party won just under 1 million votes, only 300,000 off the Bloc, yet the Greens won no seats.

Fair Vote Canada analyzed the 2008 popular vote and recalculated what the seat count would have been under proportional representation. The Conservatives would have won the most seats at 117, but not the 143 they won under FPTP. The Liberal seat count would have gone up to 81 seats, instead of their current 76. The NDP would have been big winner in the improved system with 57 seats, instead of 37, while the Bloc would have seen a reduced representation with 28 seats instead of 50, and, of course, the Greens would have won 23 seats.[3]

A further irony of the 2008 election was that, due to the all-time low voter turnout, the Conservatives won more seats with fewer votes than in 2006. The actual number of Canadians voting Conservative dropped by approximately 170,000 voters. Yet, Mr. Harper referred to the 2008 election results as giving him a "strengthened minority." In fact, the only party to receive more votes in 2008 than in 2006 was the Green Party. In 2008, Green candidates received about 270,000 more votes than in 2006.

The FPTP system is inherently unfair. The primary victim of this unfairness is not political parties, although the NDP and Greens have the largest reasons for complaint.

The Bloc Québécois and early Reform Party benefited from its impacts. Any political platform that has the tendency of concentrating votes in one region will get a real boost under FPTP.

The real victim of this electoral system is the voter. In a FPTP system it is simply not possible to say that every vote counts. Not surprisingly, following every election that produces a perverse result, the call increases for proportional representation. With the 2008 election producing a minority government with significant under-representation for the NDP and the Green Party, the demand for proportional representation began immediately. In a poll conducted during the fall of 2008, Angus Reid found that 47 percent of Canadians are ready to consider a system other than FPTP. While 33 percent of voters believe that the current system is best, 28 percent favoured proportional representation in a pure form and 19 percent liked the hybrid approach which would allocate some seats on a constituency basis, and others by proportional representation.[4]

The problems of lower voter turnout and increased voter cynicism can be confronted by changing to proportional representation. As noted in earlier chapters, those nations with PR systems experience higher voter turnout than Canada. They also enjoy a high level of satisfaction with the effectiveness of their participation. Canadian results show that voters have a very low level of satisfaction and many voters feel that their vote makes no difference to the outcome. Indeed, it is quite common to meet people who have never once in their lives voted for a candidate who has won. A Conservative in Ottawa–Vanier would share this experience with a Liberal in Calgary Centre, a New Democrat in Charlottetown, or a Green voter anywhere.

Those voters who are keenly aware of how FPTP works are increasingly motivated to vote *against* a party, rather than to vote *for* one. They realize that a vote for the candidate and party they most favour could lead to the perverse result of electing a government they actually actively don't want, by splitting the overall vote with a less dreadful choice. Voters hold their noses and vote for the "lesser of two evils," with the sad result of being forced into the choice between "the evil of two lessers."

Voting strategically is part and parcel of the FPTP system. In the 2008 election it attracted websites, such as Vote for the Environment, and even a provincial premier's campaign. Newfoundland and Labrador Premier Danny Williams, a Conservative himself, so distrusts Conservative Prime Minister Stephen Harper that he successfully ran an "ABC" campaign – Anything But Conservative. No Conservatives were elected in Newfoundland and Labrador.

Media coverage in the 2008 election posited that I supported strategic voting, which in fact I never have. I was responsible for some of this confusion. I was (and am) unwilling to criticize citizens who are making a deeply personal and important choice about how they cast their vote.

I was also unwilling to pretend that I thought all the other parties' policies were equally bad. The Conservative Party's policies were far and away the most dangerous on the climate issue, the least progressive in addressing issues of poverty and inequality, and most irresponsible in dealing with the economy. My refusal to condemn those who felt compelled to vote strategically led to my position being misreported, and then, like a bad game of telephone, the misreporting was amplified. A low ebb for me was looking up at a TV screen in a local nursing home where I was visiting a friend, days before the election. Catching my name, I saw the "crawl" along the bottom of CTV NewsNet proclaiming I had urged people to vote Liberal! The communications arm of Stephen Harper's campaign was once again hard at work inventing the news.

I do not support any call to "vote strategically" because it encourages voting from fear and distrust. It calls on people to vote out of negativity. And, tragically, it leads voters to make the wrong choices, because it is impossible to know which vote is the "strategic vote." Those who might want to elect an NDP MP may feel compelled to vote Liberal to stop a Conservative. If they have guessed wrong, they may have cost the NDP critical winning votes. Green supporters always know it is an uphill struggle to elect an MP, but if enough of those supporters voted Green, a Green MP could be (and eventually will be) elected. Still, for some voters, in the FPTP system, the multiple reasons for voting for the policies you want will always be trumped by voting for policies you think you can tolerate.

The most effective way to enliven democracy and give citizens the power of voting for the future they want is to support the change to proportional representation.

Many prominent Canadians support the call for proportional representation. Fair Vote Canada boasts a non-partisan advisory board including Conservative Senator Hugh Segal, former Liberal Cabinet member Lloyd Axworthy, former NDP leader Ed Broadbent, leading former senior civil servants Sylvia Ostrey and Tom Kent, among a bevy of other prominent Canadians – including David Suzuki, Maude Barlow, and Robert Bateman. Former Progressive Conservative MP Patrick Boyer, who is also a member of the Fair Vote advisory board, has written: "The situation in Canada's legislatures today certainly demands a fresh look at proportional representation. No matter what some may smugly say about the 'instability' of other countries' parliaments . . . we have a duty now to move forward. The degree of partyism in Parliament and the legislatures this last decade of the twentieth century makes a sham of our pretence of having effective, democratic, representative democracy."[5]

Some politicians seem to align themselves with the call for reform early in their careers, only to abandon it once in power. That list includes Jean Chrétien, who called for proportional representation when he was running for leader of the Liberal Party in 1984, but forgot about it once he gained leadership.[6] Stephen Harper once co-wrote an academic paper calling for proportional representation. Jack Layton and the NDP have PR as an official part of their platform but never pressed it when opportunities to do so presented themselves in negotiations with the Liberal minority government of Paul Martin.

Stephen Harper and I discussed the potential for reforming the voting system on a phone call back in September 2006. He made the call to congratulate me for winning the Green Party leadership. In hopes of finding an area of constructive cooperation, I asked if he would be willing to pursue proportional representation. He acknowledged that he had once advocated it, but then said, in a very economical statement of the problem, "No group of elected representatives is likely to fundamentally change the system by which they were elected."

This may seem like a truism, but that does not mean it is universally true. In fact, in New Zealand parliamentarians did change the system. In the 1990s, they rejected FPTP and embraced a more proportional voting system.

The situation that propelled the shift to proportional representation in New Zealand is not that dissimilar from what we are experiencing in Canada. Like Canada, New Zealand is a Commonwealth nation, a constitutional monarchy with a parliamentary democracy. Like Canada, New Zealand has a significant challenge to respect and engage the indigenous people, the Maori, in their democracy. Like Canada, New Zealand had inherited an archaic voting system from England.

The impetus for change in New Zealand came from successive elections delivering false-majority governments. In both 1978 and 1981, the National Party had won the majority of seats but the Labour Party had actually won more votes. The third party, the Social Credit Party, had won a large percentage of the vote (16 percent and 21 percent respectively), but had seen that translate into only one and then two seats. The Labour Party managed to get elected in 1984 and instituted a Royal Commission to examine the electoral system. It reported in 1986 with a document still referenced in the New Zealand press to this day, entitled *Towards a Better Democracy*. In 2002, the judge who chaired the commission, Mr. Justice John Wallace, reflected on the process, and his doubts that such a major change in the voting system could be accepted:

> Indeed, at the time of the Royal Commission Report, there were very few instances of a country making a major change to its electoral system in other than revolutionary, or near revolutionary circumstances . . .
>
> We ultimately decided to recommend MMP (mixed member proportional), that is, the German voting system, with a limited number of modifications to suit New Zealand's specific needs. I personally

thought it might be a decade before one or other of the main political parties decided to hold a referendum; and that if this happened it would be as a result of voters becoming more and more unhappy about the capricious aspects of FPP [first past the post] in an increasingly diverse electorate, which also wished to see a more representative Parliament. In the event, and for a variety of reasons, the two referendums (the first to choose the preferred new system and the second to determine whether voters wanted to adopt the new system or to stay with FPP), came sooner than I expected.[7]

It did indeed. The public pressure for change, and the lively discussion engendered by the Royal Commission report, led to a National Party election promise to allow a citizens' referendum on changing the voting system. Wisely, they undertook two separate referenda. The first was to resolve the question of whether the voters wanted a new system and to opt for one in particular. The second was to choose between keeping First Past the Post or moving to the preferred option chosen by the previous referendum. In 1993 – just seven years after the Royal Commission report – the second referendum was held leading to the change in voting systems. The Royal Commission had recommended that the change be approved by a simple majority of the voters. By a margin of 53.9 percent to 46.1 percent, New

Zealand voters decided to stop electing their members of Parliament exclusively by First Past the Post.

The system they approved, as noted above, was based on the German model. A pure PR system would allow a vote purely based on party preference, without the need to have a representative from a local area. Germany, like many countries with some form of PR, is more of a hybrid. Some members of the national parliament are elected as local representatives, while others are elected based on the support nationally for their party. The system New Zealanders chose is generally known as Mixed Member Proportional (MMP).

In New Zealand, as in Germany and elsewhere, every voter gets two votes. One is applied to a local candidate whose election is still based on First Past the Post and the other is applied to a national party. The seats in Parliament are allocated based on the proportion of the vote that actually goes to each party. If there are not enough MPs elected through the local vote count to reflect that party's percentage of the national vote, that party gets additional seats from its national party list to get to a fair result. In other words, candidates on a national party list "top up" the parliamentary numbers of the locally elected MPs until the party balance in the Parliament reflects the overall popular vote. If a party does not win at least 5 percent of the popular vote, it is not entitled to any seats from the national party list.

The New Zealand experience is worth studying. The national debate about the change was intense. Anti-MMP forces organized. In order to accommodate the changes, the size of the New Zealand Parliament grew from ninety-nine members to 120. This aspect of the change was quite unpopular. Justice Wallace, in reflecting on the key determinants that carried the day for MMP, highlighted correcting the power imbalance that was occurring in the New Zealand Parliament. It is this observation that strikes a strong chord for those worried that our current system is moving to an overly centralized PMO-run government: "In particular, voters wanted to increase the representativeness of Parliament and also to introduce greater checks and balances in our unicameral system which, under FPP, enabled a large Cabinet to dominate caucus, with Cabinet itself often being heavily under the influence of the Prime Minister and other powerful figures."[8]

They succeeded in changing the voting system, but not without hiccoughs. There was some consternation when voters realized they would not know who had "won" the election for some time.

The public, despite pre-election warnings of the high likelihood that a government would not be known on election night, and despite this having occurred in several relatively recent elections under FPP (for example, 1981 and 1993), were surprised and disconcerted by

the time involved, which in some other countries with
a proportional system would not be thought unduly
lengthy. Thus, in the Netherlands, the average time for
formation of a government is nine weeks and three
days, in Belgium five weeks, and in Germany three
weeks and one day.[9]

Without First Past the Post, forming a government actually took some time. There were no majority governments.
Instead minority parliaments worked to negotiate coalition arrangements. However, these have worked quite
well. Budgets have been passed and legislation achieved.
Effective government, one of the Royal Commission's key
goals, appears to have been realized under MMP. There is
far greater consultation and cooperation between parties,
and no government has risked being defeated by a vote of
non-confidence.

As well, there is far less voter dissatisfaction over
"orphaned votes." The goal of seeing a more diverse House
of Commons has also been achieved. The biggest increase
has been in indigenous Maori MPs, whose number has
more than doubled. The proportion of women in the
House has also increased, and Asian members have been
elected for the first time. After four general elections, New
Zealand is still learning to adapt to the new system.

There are many kinds of proportional voting systems,
and they all share two characteristics in contrast with the

status quo: they are both fairer and far are more complicated to explain than First Past the Post. One of the other
popular front-runners for countries moving away from
FPTP has been a system of preferential voting called STV,
or Single Transferable Vote. The approach taken with a single
transferable vote is to keep the process as close as possible
to the existing practice of voting for a candidate – as
opposed to a party. In order to make it fairer, a group of
local ridings or districts is pooled together. The candidates'
names are on the ballot and each voter gets to vote in order
of preference for a number of potential MPs. STV has been
brought in in other Commonwealth nations used to the
FPTP system. It is used for the Australian Senate, and for
both houses in Ireland and Tasmania. It is more complicated
to explain than to cast an STV ballot.

Under STV, a voter gets a single ballot, but multiple
choices. The voter ranks his or her preference among a
group of candidates from a cluster of districts. When the
votes are counted, the votes for the most popular candidates are clear. Once elected, any more votes for those
elected candidates as "first choice" continue to be counted
toward the "second choice." The lower-tier vote preferences are tallied up. The result is a much fairer distribution
of votes to candidates who are local, but whose election
has ensured a fair distribution of support among a number
of choices. As described by Canadian writer Nick Loenen,
who supports the STV approach,

> It should . . . be noted that lower preferences cannot
> hurt a voter's higher preferences, since the lower do
> not take effect until the higher preferences have either
> been elected or eliminated . . .
>
> Expressing a preference for a particular candidate,
> party, platform or local issue does not compel the voter
> to reject outright all other options . . . Instead of out-
> right approval or rejection, preference voting is like
> asking voters to register their likes and dislikes on a scale
> of one to ten. Preference voting registers the degree of
> support present among all voters for candidates, parties,
> and issues with exceptional precision . . . Citizens' par-
> ticipation becomes more meaningful and significant.[10]

The STV system offers the voter even more choice than
the two-vote Mixed Member Proportional system. Both
are huge improvements over our current archaic "winner
take all" approach.

Canadians, particularly in Ontario and British
Columbia, will be very familiar with the debates over these
two options. British Columbians narrowly missed the
chance to implement STV in a 2005 referendum. It was
determined that a simple majority would not be sufficient
to consider STV approved and the government set out a
requirement for STV to obtain at least 60 percent of the
vote before it could be enacted. STV missed narrowly
when 57.69 percent of the voters supported it. The issue

will be on the ballot in B.C. again on May 12, 2009. For the sake of fairer voting, all Canadians should thank B.C. voters if they accept STV.

Ontario voters were less warm to MMP, which was on the ballot in the October 2007 provincial election. Ontario voters went to the polls to elect a new roster of members to Queen's Park at the same time they voted on the MMP question. The approval required was double-barrelled: it had to pass with more than a majority and with regional balance. In the event, 63 percent of voters voted against the change to MMP.

In analyzing Canadians' reluctance to change the voting system, there are a few lessons to be learned. A change as significant as the way citizens elect their parliaments is not undertaken lightly. In both British Columbia and Ontario the choice of the specific variety of proportional voting was determined through a citizens' assembly. It was a fair way to proceed and, indeed, is what Green Party policy advocates for Canada. However, it is likely that the New Zealand approach of a Royal Commission actively engaged more citizens and obtained a higher level of media coverage with attendant public awareness. In Ontario, on the eve of the MMP referendum, two different polls showed that only about half of voters even knew a referendum was taking place.[11] All told, the New Zealand Royal Commission received over 800 submissions and took two years to come to fruition. The commission may have done a better job in preparing the ground for real change than our citizens' assemblies.

It was also likely a huge advantage to the success of the New Zealand vote that the referendum occurred in two stages. When a very complicated proposal is put forward requiring a large plurality in order to reject the status quo, it is unlikely to succeed. By splitting the question in two, assessing initially either support for the specific proposal in question or willingness to move to a specific proposal, and subsequently voting on the actual change, the level of preparedness and acceptance for change is raised.

In the wake of the poor result in Ontario for MMP, the quality of the information made available by the government was identified as a critical flaw. Many Ontarians believed the MMP system was just poorly explained. As well, some felt the referendum on changing the voting system should not have been held in conjunction with the provincial election.

Ed Broadbent, former leader of the federal NDP, was particularly outspoken in criticizing the failings of the campaign for MMP and the level of government support to communicate the proposal. "I condemn the government of Ontario for not making adequate resources available to inform the people of Ontario what this would mean for them if they voted for it," Mr. Broadbent told the *Ottawa Citizen*.[12]

As in New Zealand, the change to MMP would have required a larger legislative assembly. And, as in New

Zealand, this proved a hard sell in Ontario. With only $6.8 million allocated to the public education campaign, simply not enough resources were dedicated to the effort. When half the voters didn't even know the issue would be included on the ballot, the critics were probably correct in faulting the effort to communicate. Still, it may be that more than one referendum will always be needed for voters to change the old and familiar, even if they wish they could.

In any future national referendum, it is critical that the ballot question be in two parts, if we wish to resolve our "electoral dysfunction" – as *Royal Canadian Air Farce* comic Don Ferguson describes it in a video on the Fair Vote Canada website.

Part one could be a simple "Do you favour the existing system for electing MPs, known as 'First Past the Post'?" Part two could pursue the matter, asking "If the voting system is changed, would you prefer an STV or an MMP approach?" In this way, if there is no clear move for STV or MMP, question one would at least gauge the level of public support for the current system. In recent polling, the greatest support for FPTP came from Conservative voters, while the greatest support for proportional representation was from NDP and Green voters.[13]

Informed public debate and discussion is the first step. Driving that discussion will be the level of citizen dissatisfaction with the existing system. In that light, we should all be grateful for the nasty mess of the fall 2008 thirteen-day session of Parliament. The threatened vote of non-confidence in a government that did not receive support from 62 percent of Canadians might just set the stage for real change. In some ways, it already has.

Chapter 9

Coalitions as the Way of the Future

WHEN I BEGAN RESEARCHING and writing this book, I had no idea that the newly re-elected minority government of Stephen Harper was about to demonstrate the truth of a number of its key points. The fateful and ill-considered attempt, in November 2008, to skewer the opposition parties under the cover of an economic statement created one of the most unpredictable series of events in modern Canadian political history.

The crisis was as dramatic as it was unexpected. Following the October election, much was said about Stephen Harper's "new approach." The changes in Cabinet responsibility, particularly replacing Peter Van Loan as House leader with Jay Hill, combined with friendly outreach to other party leaders and premiers, was said to bode well for a more cooperative Parliament. Political scientists and media commentators were persuaded that Harper had learned the lessons of governing as a minority. Antonia Maioni, political scientist and director of the McGill Institute for the Study of Canada, was interviewed by the *Globe and Mail* and joined the general consensus that the fall 2008 session of Parliament would rise above the acrimony of the previous session: "Stephen Harper is realizing that he is a minority government prime minister . . . I think he realizes that he has to find new strategies to govern. He may be coming to terms with that as a political leader."[1]

Based on this and other interviews with "senior Tory sources," the *Globe* concluded: "After three years of leading one of the most combative federal governments in recent memory, Stephen Harper is telling his MPs that it's time they take the high road. MPs and officials across government were given marching orders by the Prime Minister recently and told to shelve the aggressive ways of the first term in favour of a kinder, gentler attitude."[2]

I was in the House for the opening day of the November 2008 Parliament, and in the Senate chamber for the Speech from the Throne. There was goodwill in the air, but by the first day of Question Period, it had evaporated. The heckling and the rudeness seemed only slightly less awful than during the previous session.

Less than eight days later, it was clear the there was no "kinder, gentler approach." Instead, there was a ruthless attempt to strike a fatal financial blow to the opposition parties as they faced their post-election debts. The dramatic events following the November 27, 2008 economic update underscored the extent to which many Canadians do not really grasp the differences between parliamentary democracy within a constitutional monarchy and the American republic's electoral system. The person who displayed the most ignorance about our system was the prime minister himself, although his statements fell into the category of deliberate disinformation more than a lack of knowledge.

The parliamentary uproar established once again that a minority government is vulnerable and must consult opposition parties. The somewhat archaic expression that the governing party must "enjoy the confidence of the House" became tangibly real. One could almost hear the trust and toleration for parties of opposing viewpoints come tumbling down even as Finance Minister Jim Flaherty's voice still echoed in the chamber.

Flaherty was reported to have been reluctant to take the approach demanded by his prime minister. Just days earlier, the prime minister had spoken at the APEC forum in Peru and made clear that in the context of a global financial crisis, a credit crunch, and a looming recession, deficit financing was now a "necessity." Harper spoke of the need for a stimulus package. Yet on November 27 his finance minister read a projection for budgetary surpluses — which appeared to anyone familiar with the situation to be imaginary — and called for austerity. There would no stimulus to the economy in the form of government spending at least in the short term, which is when the country needed it most. Wrapped in the austerity message was the *coup de grâce* — an attempt to bankrupt opposition parties by removing the per vote subsidy instituted as a reform under Prime Minister Chrétien.

The attack on taxpayer funding to political parties was nearly irresistible to the Harper–Flanagan long-term strategy. Conservative strategist Tom Flanagan had suggested that the conflict between the two major parties in Canada was akin to the Punic Wars. In a column in the *Globe and Mail* on August 28, 2008, he wrote:

> Do you remember your ancient history? From a Conservative point of view, this is a rerun of the Punic Wars, with the Conservatives starring as the rising Roman republic and the Liberals as the evil empire of Carthage . . . and in the third [Punic War] they defeated Carthage totally, razed the city to the ground and sowed the salt in the fields so nothing would ever grow their again . . . Destruction of the Liberals is not at hand . . . But . . . they . . . could be pushed into a financial pit they can never climb out of.[3]

The financial destruction of the official opposition could hardly be called part of a "hidden agenda" with open advocacy of the political equivalent of a scorched earth policy. Conservative strategists must have been certain that many

Canadians would be shocked to find that political parties received any taxpayer funding. In fact, the polls in newspapers (unscientific, as they required people to vote on websites) ran largely against the continuation of this funding. Only some commentators, such as Jeffrey Simpson writing in the *Globe,* placed the per vote subsidy in the context of financing reform. "Canadians fought a long battle to get these inducements for people to give to political parties; they can't let one party's naked self-interest push back progress."[4]

It was that aspect of "naked self-interest," especially when set in contrast to a looming economic downturn requiring government action, that destroyed any potential for the opposition parties to be able to work with the Harper government.

Don Martin in the *National Post* put it this way: "This showdown [is] an unforgivable breach of the trust voters bestowed on Harper. He was elected to lead a minority government with a spirit of co-operation. He thought he had set a deadly trap for his opponents. He may well find himself as the victim."[5]

All in one blow, Harper had dealt a nearly mortal injury to his own minority government. Counting on a supine opposition, relying on their fear of provoking an election so quickly after the October 14 vote, Harper badly misjudged the potential reaction.

Within hours it was clear that he had prompted a unanimous determination of the opposition members to defeat his government on a confidence motion. The Liberals, the New Democrats, and the Bloc could not agree to vote for such an economic statement. Even Independent MP and former Conservative Bill Casey issued a press release stating that he would vote non-confidence. The opposition leaders did what they should do in a parliamentary democracy: they attempted to find a way to present the governor general with an alternative to another federal general election. They decided to see if there was a way they could work together and offer the governor general an option for a government run as a coalition.

There was a clear willingness to defeat the government within days. A confidence vote loomed for Monday, December 1. Prime Minister Harper acted quickly, starting to withdraw some elements of the economic statement, backtracking on the threat to political party financing and altering the parliamentary calendar to delay the non-confidence vote by one week. He announced the vote would be a full seven days later – on December 8. The opposition parties were not to be bullied and had done the unthinkable. Bridging their differences in an agreement to run a Liberal–NDP coalition government, with a commitment from the Bloc Québécois to avoid non-confidence votes on an agreed list of subjects, the opposition leaders signalled their preparedness to go to the governor general and offer to form the government. The Green Party of Canada expressed support as well, recognizing that such an arrangement would better reflect the way the majority of Canadians had voted, including the nearly 1 million people who had voted Green.

In Canada, the formation of a coalition government once the minority government has lost the confidence of the House is not only legal and constitutional; it reflects maturity and willingness to work in a cooperative fashion. It creates the opportunity for a return to a true parliamentary democracy in which all the members of Parliament, in a representative assembly, can offer the monarch and the public the best way forward. Certainly, such a coalition could not survive if its prime minister were to act unilaterally. Cabinet members drawn from different parties would demand freedom of action in their sphere of responsibility. The power of party loyalties and discipline would be blunted by the sharing of power.

What was striking about the events of late 2008 was the ease with which Stephen Harper, with his usual accomplices in the media, turned his egregious act of bare-knuckled political opportunism into a "power grab" by opposition leaders. The Conservative communication strategy was aided by the frequency with which news reports referred to a "constitutional crisis." Actually, there was only one crisis – the one impacting the fortunes of Harper's minority government. If the normal non-confidence process was followed, the government would lose the vote on December 8, and the governor general would have two options: allow the Liberal–NDP coalition a chance to govern or call an election. Neither outcome was, in any sense, a "constitutional crisis."

Some in the media, particularly in the CBC, ran what amounted to helpful "crash courses" in parliamentary democracy. Experts in constitutional monarchies and their constitutions were interviewed, and they explained that the replacement of a minority government that had lost the confidence of the House with a coalition was legal and constitutional. In fairness, even some of those most reliably in Harper's corner expressed the consensus view that he had blundered badly in provoking the threat to the survival of his government.

Harper would have none of it. He had two cards and he played them aggressively. He tried to shift attention from his own actions by claiming that the coalition was attempting an antidemocratic power grab and that it lacked legitimacy because of its reliance on the Bloc. He, his Conservative MPs, and their supportive talk radio hosts across Canada described it as a "separatist coalition," as though somehow the coalition aided the separatist cause. This was demonstrably false. Not one item in the agreement securing the Bloc's support on a range of actions assisted the sovereigntist movement. The coalition's agenda in no way hurt Canadian unity.

The attacks on the coalition as "separatist" risked turning Harper's political problems into a national unity crisis. The West was enraged and anger was mounting. Meanwhile, many Quebecers who had voted for the Bloc, and even those who had not, were offended that Harper had decided that only some MPs really mattered in the House. And some were, apparently, Untouchables. Conservative MPs in the House yelled "treason" and "traitor" across the aisle at opposition members. It was ugly and getting uglier.

Bloc Leader Gilles Duceppe gamely produced and read into *Hansard* the September 9, 2004 letter Harper had co-signed with Jack Layton and Duceppe offering the same possibility to Governor General Adrienne Clarkson when they had hoped to bring down the minority government of Paul Martin. It read:

> As leaders of the opposition parties, we are well aware that, given the Liberal minority government, you could be asked by the Prime Minister to dissolve the 38th Parliament at any time should the House of Commons fail to support some part of the government's program. We respectfully point out that the opposition parties, who together constitute a majority in the House, have been in close consultation. We believe that, should a request for dissolution arise this should give you cause, as constitutional practice has determined, to consult the opposition leaders and consider all of your options before exercising your constitutional authority. Your attention to this matter is appreciated.[6]

Despite the existence of a letter clearly demonstrating that Harper had been prepared to work closely with the Bloc and obtain power through such cooperation, Harper claimed that this plan was somehow entirely different from what was now being proposed. In fact, the Conservative minority government had relied on the Bloc's support dozens of times. In order to hang on to power, the PM was prepared to trash all the progress he had made for his party in Quebec. And he was prepared to create national divisions even as the nation faced its most serious economic challenge in decades.

Harper blasted the coalition and its leader, outgoing Liberal Leader Stéphane Dion, saying, "The opposition has every right to defeat the government but Stéphane Dion does not have the right to take power without an election."[7] He gave that message repeatedly, going so far as to describe the coalition plan as one to "overturn the results of the election" or even worse, as a *coup d'état*. Of course, this was dangerous nonsense. There was every right for members of Parliament to cobble together a new government once Harper's party, having a minority of seats, had lost the confidence of the House.

Nevertheless, Harper's incendiary language had the desired effect. Public opinion polls showed that at least half of Canadians, or more than had voted Conservative, agreed there was something illegitimate and undemocratic in the coalition's plans. Dennis Pilon, a political scientist at the University of Victoria, commented, "I do not mean to be alarmist in suggesting that we may be heading for violence. But the actions of this prime minister are coming dangerously close to inciting mob rule."[8]

In this climate, Stephen Harper prepared to seek an unprecedented prorogation of the House. Never in Canadian history had a prime minister asked a governor general to end a session of Parliament within days of its opening. Never in the history of modern parliamentary democracies anywhere in the world had a prime minister sought to close down the government to avoid losing a confidence vote.

Had Prime Minister Paul Martin tried such a move to avoid the non-confidence vote on November 28, 2005, when his government fell, Opposition Leader Stephen Harper would have been incensed at such antidemocratic gall. In fact, in reference to Martin's minority back in the fall of 2004, Stephen Harper had said: "When a government starts trying to cancel dissent or avoid dissent is frankly when it's rapidly losing its moral authority to govern."[9]

On December 4, 2008, after a two-hour private meeting with Governor General Michaëlle Jean, the prime minister emerged from Rideau Hall. As the sky darkened and a hail storm began, he announced the House was pro-rogued. This move was breathtakingly antidemocratic. The business of the people in the House of Commons was shut down to protect the life of a minority government.

Surprisingly, public reaction was for the most part

quite muted. As Lawrence Martin wrote in the *Globe:* "The Harper government did a spectacular job of turning public opinion in its favour with its separatists-at-the-gates fear-mongering. Opposed to the option of a coalition government, the public then welcomed, only two weeks after Parliament had begun, her prorogation."[10]

This was aided by the underlying unfamiliarity with our parliamentary system. As noted earlier, the Dominion Institute conducted a poll in this period and discovered that 51 percent of Canadians believed that we, like the Americans, hold a direct election for the position of head of government.[11]

But that is not to say that there was no anger. Ronald Wright, best-selling author of *A Short History of Progress,* wrote:

> Modern parliamentary democracy rests on a single great principle: The government must have the consent of the governed. This consent is delegated by the people to their MPs. The government must then be able to carry the "confidence" of the House of Commons. Majority governments rarely lose that confidence; minority governments often do. When the government cannot carry the House, it falls.
>
> Suspending Parliament to dodge a vote the government fears it will lose is so deeply undemocratic, it should never have been mooted by politicians, the

media or the Governor General. The English Civil War was fought on this very issue – after King Charles I shut down Parliament when he found its restrictions uncongenial. The King lost his head.

We no longer behead people in Canada, but Stephen Harper's *coup d'état* cannot be allowed to stand, not least because of the precedent. Any future government can now slip the leash of democracy in the same way. This is how constitutions fail.[12]

Wright's concerns were echoed by constitutional law expert Errol Mendes of the University of Ottawa: "This is a major constitutional precedent and that worries me more than anything else. . . . Any time that the prime minister wants to evade the confidence of the House now he can use this precedent to do so."[13]

Former Commissioner of Official Languages Keith Spicer was blunter: "Finally, the world pays a little attention to Canada. And what does it see? Zimbabwe run by the Queen."[14]

One political scientist can be credited with nearly psychic powers: Peter Russell whose *Two Cheers for Minority Government: The Evolution of Canadian Parliamentary Democracy,* published earlier in 2008, made the case for reinventing the way Parliament works in light of the likelihood that Canada will be governed by minorities with greater frequency in the future. Russell's thesis is that far from fearing minority governments, Canadians should embrace them. In canvassing the dozen Canadian minority federal governments, Russell judges them largely successful in accomplishing their ends. He also sees enormous risks in the centralization of power in the PMO and the potential for false majorities. The solution is, of course, proportional representation, but under the status quo, Russell argues that we should be able to evolve toward more cooperative minority Parliaments.

The growing likelihood of minority Parliaments should encourage greater cooperation in the House of Commons. One of the great benefits of evolving in this direction would be to reduce the partisanship of the House. Russell identifies political parties as a major culprit in the erosion of parliamentary democracy through the concentration of power in a prime ministerial government.

> In the modern era, a number of factors have combined to make this fusion of powers a real and present danger to the democratic capacity of parliamentary government. *First and foremost among these is the emergence of disciplined and well-financed political parties* whose leaders employ the techniques of mass advertising to win and retain power. This development is aided and abetted by techniques of public management that downplay the deliberative role of elected representatives and Parliament's role in holding government responsible for its decisions. [emphasis added][15]

Political parties are healthy in a democracy. Any citizen can join a party and, in a representative and grassroots party, any member can play a role in developing party policy. The problem is that the goals of political parties are not necessarily public policy goals. They tend to be all about one thing – getting and retaining power. When the party that forms government decides that governing is less important than winning the next election, the entire parliamentary process becomes a mere backdrop for non-stop electioneering.

While political parties wield great power in our democracy, the vast majority of Canadians report that they have never been members of political parties. The number of those who have never had involvement with political parties has increased in the last three years from 74 to 85 percent.[16] There is something ironic about a situation where political parties have such power in a democracy, yet 85 percent of the voters are not willing to join any party.

The insidious nature of partisanship is daunting. To be engaged in partisan politics is by definition to "take sides." I had long been attracted to the non-partisan politics of the German Green Party. Founder Petra Kelly used to refer to her party as the "anti-party party."[17] There will likely not be another party with as large a commitment to planetary survival and the common good as the Green Party of Canada. Nevertheless, some Green Party members would rather that I toed the line of conventional party politics. There are clear expectations and unwritten rules in politics, and the media and party members demand that politicians stay within those rules.

In Canada, the old and safe route is to beat up on all the other parties (constantly) while pointing out that only your party is virtuous. It shows the proper team spirit: my team versus your team. Sports analogies abound. In fact, many politicians and commentators refer to politics as a "blood sport." I once made the mistake of referring to the hatred of party versus party as "tribalism," only to be upbraided for giving offence to indigenous peoples, but it is hard to find another word that so captures the intensity and irrationality of these ancient rivalries.

In the last few years, as leader of the Green Party, I have tried to engage other parties in cooperative approaches to meet the goals of protecting the planet from the imminent ravages of the climate crisis. Stéphane Dion was the only other political leader willing to think of new ways to cooperate across party lines. When I spoke to friends in the New Democratic Party, it was always clear that the thought of working with the Liberals was anathema to them. Even when they were asked if it would not be better to cooperate in the short term to avoid hitting tipping points in the atmosphere and unleashing devastating climatic impacts, their response was virulent. I am not sufficiently partisan to understand why sensible people would not be willing to work together in the interests of protecting future generations.

Constantly attacking the other parties is a nice simple message. The media understand what you are doing. Doing something different is threatening to the whole construct of partisanship. A political party leader's job is to advance partisan advantage at all times.

The problem is that while party members may love this approach, the voters do not like it. Voters know it is a lot of stuff and nonsense. What the majority of Canadians would like is a way to see their views and values reflected in the House of Commons that is actually elected.

The power of political parties and the cult of leadership it has brought to Canadian political life all militate against greater cooperation. To cooperate one day is to invite a conclusion the next day that you have been weak. Partisanship works against the notion "You can accomplish anything you want if you don't care who gets the credit." That ethic captures the spirit that Tommy Douglas brought to politics. His willingness to cooperate to bring in universal health care is now celebrated, but I have my doubts such behaviour could ever surface in the current atmosphere of toxic partisanship that demands that politicians try to get all the credit all the time for everything.

In *Two Cheers for Minority Government*, Peter Russell argues persuasively for greater stabilization of minority parliaments, through fixed election dates, greater cooperation between parties, and resort to coalition governments. His ideas made sense as I read them, but as a matter of "evolution" they seem beyond the reach of the current Canadian political culture.

Great moments of flux and crisis allow innovations to occur. The fact is that the prime minister lost the confidence of the House in December 2008, whether or not the matter was put to a vote. His spectacular miscalculation led to something that would have been impossible to imagine even weeks earlier. Arch-enemies put aside their distrust and ancient hatreds. The Bloc has an intense dislike for Stéphane Dion, who, as champion of federalism, was the author of the *Clarity Act*. Stéphane Dion has always been similarly hostile to the Bloc. Once when he was environment minister, I had made the mistake of suggesting to him that he solicit the Bloc's help on Kyoto; his reaction was apoplectic. Now, here was Dion ready to work with Duceppe. And more amazing, Jack Layton was prepared to assist a Liberal to become prime minister. The NDP's hatred of Liberals was once described to me by an NDP friend who labels himself as a "fundamentalist." No matter how much it might make sense to cooperate, he assured me, NDPers could never and would never cooperate with Liberals. A coalition was simply the stuff of fantasy only days before it became a reality.

The Conservative communication machine would have the public believe that this willingness to cooperate was simply a "power grab," but that is demonstrably not the case. If that was all that was at play, Harper's government would not have survived from January 2006 to fall 2008.

At any time in that two-and-a-half-year period, the same opposition leaders could have formed a coalition.

The willingness to work together in a coalition government was born of necessity. There was no way to trust Harper any longer. His willingness to ignore the nation's economic woes and to bankrupt his political opponents was beyond the pale. No minority prime minister had ever displayed such contempt so soon after an election. It was the perfect storm for a new type of parliamentary approach to emerge.

Canada has known only a few coalition governments. The first predates Canada. It was the "Great Coalition" of 1864–67 that allowed Upper and Lower Canada to find common ground and form the nation. Several parties, George Brown's "Clear Grits," George-Etienne Cartier's Parti bleu, and John A. Macdonald's Liberal-Conservatives, joined in the effort. The result was Canada.

A coalition government did not surface in Canada again until the First World War. In 1917 a Unionist federal government formed under Robert Borden. It was a coalition because the opposition Liberals under Laurier split over the issue of conscription. Some Liberals who favoured conscription joined with the Unionist MPs. The pro-conscription forces, Liberals and Unionists, chose not to run against each other in the 1917 election. They won by a landslide and governed until 1919. In a dispute over tariffs a number of Unionist MPs resigned, and the remaining Unionists were able to continue to govern until the election of 1921.

Older Canadians will recall that Winston Churchill led a Liberal–Labour coalition to victory in the Second World War.

The best-known example of a successful coalition in modern Canadian politics was that of the Ontario government from 1985 to 1987. The presumed "winner" of the May 2, 1985 election was Conservative Frank Miller with 52 seats. Liberal leader David Peterson had 48 seats and the NDP had 25. On May 28, 1985, David Peterson and NDP leader Bob Rae entered into a written agreement. They agreed to a shared agenda for two years. Initially, Premier Miller did not accept the agreement, casting doubt as to its constitutional validity. The great constitutional scholars of the day supported the legality, led by Eugene Forsey, who called the arrangement "impeccable."[18] Finally, on June 19, Premier Miller submitted his resignation to the lieutenant governor and invited David Peterson to form government. The Peterson–Rae government was not a true coalition in that the NDP did not share a place at the Cabinet table, but it did influence policy.

In a less formal sense, the minority government of Pierre Trudeau in 1972 was typified by cooperation with the NDP. Liberals had 109 MPs, the Progressive Conservatives had 107, and the NDP under dynamic leader David Lewis had 31 seats. NDP support was needed to prop up the

Liberal government. Without any public acceptance of a formal relationship with the Liberals, David Lewis met frequently and privately with Deputy Prime Minister Allan J. MacEachen to negotiate policy. That minority was truly successful not in spite of the cooperation, but because of it.

Peter Russell writes that the Trudeau minority government "formed an effective legislative alliance with the NDP that accomplished a good deal, including major improvements in social security, legislation on election expenses and foreign investment, and the appointment of Justice Thomas Berger, a former leader of the NDP in British Columbia, to head the Mackenzie Valley Pipeline Inquiry."[19]

However rare in Canada, coalition governments are routine in most democracies. This is particularly true in the Nordic countries where coalitions work particularly well. Green Parties have been part of coalition governments in Sweden, Norway, and Denmark, as well as in France, Germany, Belgium, and the Netherlands, and Ireland is currently governed by a coalition. Since the acceptance of Mixed Member Proportional representation in New Zealand, Greens have supported coalitions there. The advent of MMP has brought more transparent declarations of cooperation from party leaders. The governor general of New Zealand actually asked the leaders of political parties to state publicly, in advance of the election, with which parties they would be prepared to cooperate. Although the New Zealand First Party had gone into the election suggesting it would be likely to support the Labour Party, following the first MMP election, it ended up forming a coalition government with the National Party. Despite unhappiness with this first experience, the governor general has continued to formally explore the attitudes of political party leaders to one another to be better prepared for entrusting government to ruling coalitions. (Certainly in the wake of her December 2008 to allow the prorogation of Parliament, there have been calls for greater openness and explanation from Canada's governor general.[20])

The uninformed slights against coalitions, that they are ineffective or unstable, are not borne out by experience in other parts of the world. While the Israeli Parliament, under pure proportional representation, has been fractious and coalitions difficult to hobble together, in those countries with MMP the longevity of coalition governments is impressive. In New Zealand, since the advent of MMP, coalition governments have lasted as long as governments under FPTP used to last – three years on average. In Germany and in Denmark, the average lifespan of a coalition government is impressive; forty-four and forty-one months respectively on average since 1990.

In fact, a move toward coalitions would reverse the trends that threaten Canadian democracy. Working more cooperatively would constrain excessive partisanship, rebalance the roles of individual MPs and of the Cabinet, and reduce the one-man-rule approach typified by Prime

Minister Harper's government. The democratic deficit would be reduced.

Of course not all threats to modern Canadian democracy will be solved through coalition governments, nor even through a move to proportional representation. We still have the problem of concentration of media ownership. And coalition governments within FPTP will not solve the problem of low voter turnout. Nonetheless, absent any other change in our system, the willingness to cooperate in minority government situations, to stabilize such minorities, to remove the sword of Damocles that constantly threatens an election, would provide a much-needed tonic in other areas of political life as well.

As Naomi Klein, author of *No Logo* and *Shock Doctrine*, said in a recent interview:

> What is being proposed by this coalition is much closer to representative democracy than what we have right now, which is a government that has [slightly more than] 35 per cent of the popular vote in a turnout that was historically low, of 59 per cent of Canadian voters, which means that even though the Tories won more seats they had fewer actual votes than in the last election.
>
> I think it is really important to talk about democracy, about what it actually means in this period. In some ways I think it is even more important than talking about

the policies, because our electoral system is broken. Because of the Tories' extraordinary opportunism and terrible calculation we now have an opportunity to see a better version of democracy and see more people represented in government.[21]

The possibility of a coalition government in Canada is one of the most hopeful political events in years. Although the Harper minority government has survived the budget vote of 2009, with the coalition receiving the equivalent of political last rites, the crisis of December 2008 is hugely significant nonetheless. The experience of watching the potential coalition form should make such efforts more viable in future. In the meantime, we need to pay close attention to the indicators of political health in our democracy. We have very little time to ensure that we maintain, or more accurately, that we regain, a true democracy.

The first and most critical step is to recognize that we have a problem. We need to raise the level of public awareness that our system is being altered, slowly but surely, to a prime-minister-driven House and government. Awareness of the threat to democracy must go far beyond bemoaning the fact that young people don't vote. That is the tip of the iceberg of electoral dysfunction. The most effective solution is to approve a change in how we elect members of federal and provincial parliaments. No other single step will have as many salutary impacts.

The role of the prime minister must be readjusted to "first among equals": that is, of appropriate consultation and respectful collaboration with elected members of Parliament. The concentration of power in the hands of the prime minister can best be redistributed by forcing the reduction of partisanship through cooperation.

It is inaccurate to say that Stephen Harper personally has created this nadir in our parliamentary tradition. He is merely the most recent and very worst of any Canadian prime minister in terms of his approach, but the trend began long ago and every recent PM has contributed to this concentration of power. The problem is that the architecture of PMO and PCO has been redesigned to allow prime ministers too much sway. It is unlikely that a new prime minister of any party would begin dismantling the apparatus by which power has been centralized in his or her hands. Restoring the essence of parliamentary democracy requires a change at a fundamental level. This kind of change can emerge through readjustments of the current system of multi-parties in minority governments, or more permanently through proportional representation.

While the coalition option is now more viable in Canada, there remains the large risk of a false majority government. "Government by thunderbolt" could change the fabric of Canadian society and institutions within a single mandate. The evolution of Canadian democracy could go either way — toward greater participation and engagement with more representative government or toward being a democracy in name only.

When the first step to saving democracy is awareness of the threat, the reduced capacity of an independent Canadian media is a serious liability. There are still ways to increase public awareness. We have free speech. I can write a book like this and hope it provokes discussion and debate. We are a privileged people in terms of literacy rates, economic well-being, and education. We should be capable of shaking off inertia and acting to ensure the health of our democracy but, as Jane Jacobs warned us, we cannot allow collective amnesia to cause us to forget we once had more representative systems.

Let's open the discussion. Let's engage one another, from school civic classes to the pages of the newspapers, blog sites, and Internet magazines. We can reclaim democracy. We can return power to the voters and to each of the members of Parliament we elect. Incrementally, we have lost much of what made our democracy real. To get it back, we cannot trust to the tides of time and history. To take power back into the hands of the voters, we have to get involved ourselves. Democracy is not a spectator sport.

Acknowledgements

The need for a book like this struck me within days of the election. A number of friends provided invaluable assistance in making it possible for me to write the book I felt was needed. Maude Barlow helped by connecting me with the wonderful Susan Renouf, my editor at McClelland & Stewart, and in providing great background for the chapter on media concentration. My dear friend and former press secretary, Camille Labchuk, threw herself into the task of tracking down studies and things I knew I had read, but could not recall.

Tom Axworthy and Peter Russell both read the manuscript and sent me helpful suggestions and corrections. Don Martin generously let me read the mysterious handbook for Conservative committee chairs, as well as letting me tell the story of his discovery of the document's existence. As always, my multi-talented executive assistant Debra Eindiguer helped in untold ways.

Victoria Cate, always an inspiration, helped with editing and conclusively rejecting a series of potential titles. While I still like "Canada: Banana Republic without Benefit of Fruit," I am very grateful she nixed it as a title.

Notes

CHAPTER I

1. Pericles, *Funeral Speech for Athenian War Dead* (430 B.C.E.), variously translated as "We do not simply regard a man who does not participate in the city's life as one who just minds his own business, but as one who is good for nothing." *www.rjgeib.com/thoughts/athens/athens.html*.

2. Thanks for the early British history to a marvelous and pithy text, Sir Ivor Jennings, *The Queen's Government* (London: Penguin Books, 1954).

3. David Bercuson, "1926 Voters Showed Us the Way," *Globe and Mail*, December 5, 2008.

4. Ibid.

5. John Ralston Saul, *A Fair Country: Telling Truths About Canada* (Toronto: Viking Canada, 2008).

6. Ibid., p. xii.

7. Paul Palango, *Dispersing the Fog: Inside the Secret World of Ottawa and the RCMP* (Toronto: Key Porter, 2008), p. 47.

8. Donald Savoie, *Governing from the Centre: The Concentration of Power in Canadian Politics* (Toronto: University of Toronto Press, 1999), p. 30.

9. Ibid., p. 27.

10. Tom Kent, "Turner and Pearson: Cabinet and Trade." Presentation to Politics with Purpose: Tribute to Right Honourable John N. Turner,

Centre for the Study of Democracy in the School of Public Policy at Queen's University, October 24, 2008.

11. Eddie Goldenberg, *TheWay It Works: Inside Ottawa* (Toronto: McClelland & Stewart, 2006), pp.78-79.

12. Elizabeth McInnich and Arthur Milnes, eds., *Politics of Purpose: 40th Anniversary Edition* (Kingston: School of Policy Studies, 2009), p. viii.

13. Ibid.

14. Peter Russell, *Two Cheers for Minority Government* (Toronto: Emond Montgomery, 2008), p. 108.

15. Jeffrey Simpson, *The Friendly Dictatorship* (Toronto: McClelland & Stewart, 2001), p. 4.

16. Elizabeth May, "The Saga of Bill C-30: From Clean Air to Climate Change or Not, *Policy Options*, Institute for Research on Public Policy, May 2007.

17. Ibid.

18. Gloria Galloway, "Harper's PR Aide Secretly Asks Cabinet Staff to Critique Bosses," *Globe and Mail,* November 17, 2006.

19. From my own experience writing speeches from 1986 to 1988, it was clear that ministers did not prescreen speeches with anyone. Speeches from ministers in Jean Chrétien's government without a single note are further evidence that things did not change.

20. Personal communication with an undisclosed member of the staff.

21. Personal communication with all-around wonderful public servant Ross Reid, former chief of staff to Brian Mulroney who has also served in the Newfoundland and Labrador premier's office.

22. Tonda MacCharles, "Secret $2M Project to Build New Briefing Centre Would Supplant Nearby National Press Theatre," *Toronto Star*, October 15, 2007.

23. Val Ross, "PMO Plans New Use for Site Once Intended to House Portrait Gallery," *Globe and Mail*, September 28, 2007.

24. "PM Says Elections Canada's Veil Decision Oversteps Their Jurisdiction," CanWest News Service. Sunday, September 9, 2007.

25. In his January 26, 2008 testimony to the Natural Resources Committee, Minister Tony Clement stated that he was made aware of the situation of the Chalk River shutdown on December 5. Lunn's office first received notice of the shutdown on November 22 and she

received information about the severity of the extended shutdown on November 30.

26. David Pugliese and Kathryn May, "Gag Order," *Ottawa Citizen,* September 19, 2008; Margaret Munro, "'Muzzle' Placed on Federal Scientists," *Vancouver Sun,* February 1, 2008.

CHAPTER 2

1. Lawrence Martin, "Pulling Back the Cloak from Our Powerful Clerk," *Globe and Mail,* November 13, 2008.

2. Ibid.

3. Ibid.

4. Ibid.

5. James Travers, "Tories Get Twitchy Waiting for McCain," *Toronto Star,* June 17, 2008.

6. James Travers, "Controversial Memo Slipped to Republican, Several Sources Say," *Toronto Star,* May 27, 2008.

7. Omar El Akkad, "Prime Minister's Office Kept Tight Rein on Terror File," *Globe and Mail,* September 17, 2007.

8. Tom Axworthy, Introduction to "Politics with Purpose: Tribute to Right Honourable John N. Turner," Centre for the Study of Democracy in the School of Public Policy at Queen's University, October 24, 2008.

9. R. MacGregor Dawson and W.F. Dawson, *Democratic Government in Canada* (Toronto: University of Toronto Press, 1989), revised by Norman Ward, p. 38.

10. John Turner, Keynote Address, "Politics with Purpose."

11. Elizabeth May, *Paradise Won: The Struggle to Save South Moresby* (Toronto: McClelland & Stewart, 1990).

12. The saga of the frozen cake, which, sure enough, the minister wanted produced when South Moresby had been saved, is in *Paradise Won.*

13. May, *Paradise Won,* p. 97.

14. Anne Kingston, "Could the Queen of Green Be Mean?" *Maclean's,* October 29, 2007.

15. Pacco Francoli, "Government to Address MPs' Concerns on 'Democratic Deficit,'" *The Hill Times,* April 19, 2004.

16. Canadian Press, "Harper Letter Called Kyoto 'Socialist Scheme,'" *Toronto Star*, January 30, 2007.

17. Personal notes from March 20, 2008 hearing of the Standing Committee on the Environment.

18. Kelly Patterson, "Tory Chair Storms Out of SPP Hearing; Freezing in the Dark 'Not Relevant' to Talks on Integrating with U.S.," *Ottawa Citizen*, May 11, 2007.

19. *www.harperindex.ca/ViewArticle.cfm?Ref=0032*, May 18, 2007.

20. Bea Vongdouangchanh, "House 'Committee Obstruction Manual' from the Last Parliament Will Be Refined, Improved and Will Be Back in Play," *The Hill Times,* November 10, 2008.

21. Dawson and Dawson, *Democratic Government in Canada*, p.53.

22. May, *Paradise Won*, pp. 227-28.

23. *Hansard,* Question Period, March 21, 2007.

24. May 2, 2007, in the opening question from Stéphane Dion in Question Period:

> *Hon. Stéphane Dion (Leader of the Opposition, Lib.):* Mr. Speaker, yesterday, in a desperate attempt to reconcile the irreconcilable and plug the holes in his ministers' conflicting stories, the Prime Minister again misled this House. He claimed that the Minister of Public Safety had informed this House on April 26 that Correctional Service Canada had received allegations of torture. He never did that. The Prime Minister misled this House. Why?

> *Right Hon. Stephen Harper (Prime Minister, CPC):* Mr. Speaker, I read the quote from April 26. The Minister of Public Safety can talk about that. There have been a lot of accusations of contradictions. I just have to go back to the contradiction I pointed out yesterday. Since the Leader of the Opposition now acknowledges that Elizabeth May's comments are completely inappropriate, and since she will not retract those comments, why does he believe it is still appropriate that she would be his candidate in Central Nova?

25. Preston Manning, Address to Young President's Organization – Calgary Branch, March 15, 2008.

26. Carolyn Bennett, Keynote Address, Women's Day presentation, Parkdale United, March 8, 2007.

27. The Rat Pack was composed of Liberal MPs Sheila Copps, John Nunziata, Brian Tobin, and Don Boudria.

28. Thomas S. Axworthy, "Everything Old Is New Again: Observations on Parliamentary Reform," Centre for the Study of Democracy, Queen's University Press, April 2008, Executive Summary.

CHAPTER 3

1. Warren Kinsella, *The War Room: Political Strategies for Business, NGOs, and Anyone Who Wants to Win* (Hamilton: Dundurn Press, 2007), p. 134.

2. Ibid., p. 214.

3. Glen McGregor, "Conservative Spending on Polls Hits $31-Million," Canwest News Service, December 4, 2007.

4. Ibid.

5. Ibid.

6. Michael Valpy, "What the Tories Know About You," *Globe and Mail*, September 12, 2008.

7. Ibid.

8. Admittedly the Green Party leadership race in 2006 overlapped with the Liberal race that same year.

9. William Kaplan, *A Secret Trial: Brian Mulroney, Stevie Cameron and the Public Trust* (Montreal, Kingston: McGill-Queen's University Press, 2004), p. 15; *Fifth Estate*'s investigation, "Brian Mulroney: the Unauthorized Chapter", CBC-TV, October 31, 2007; Karlheinz Schreiber's testimony to the Ethics Committee, December 11, 2007, *Hansard: www2.parl.gc.ca/HousePublications/Publication.aspx?DocId=3200276&Language=E&Mode=1&Parl=39&Ses=2*

10. David Akin, "Harper lights up his war room," *davidakin.blogware.com/blog/_archives/2008/9/7/3873753.html*, September 7, 2008

11. Andrew Mayeda, "Tories Open Campaign 'War Room,'" Canwest News, Tuesday, April 3, 2007.

12. Ibid.

13. Donald Gutsein, "The 'Flip Flop' Drumbeat: CanWest, CTV Play Along as Tories Label Dion," *The Tyee*, *thetyee.ca/Mediacheck/2007/03/26/FlipFlop/*, March 26, 2007.

14. Ibid.

15. Valpy, "What the Tories Know About You."

16. Kevin Donovan, "How Much Is Too Much?" *Toronto Star,* November 22, 2008.

17. Steven Chase, "Wary Tories Rip Dion in TV Ad Blitz" *Globe and Mail,* January 29, 2007.

18. CTV.ca news staff, "Tories Launch New Attack Ads Against Dion," *www.ctv.ca/news,* February 13, 2007.

19. CTV.ca news staff, "Tory Ad Attacks Dion's Fiscal Imbalance Stance," *www.ctv.ca/news,* April 2, 2007.

20. Canadian Press, "Tories Launch New Round of Attack Ads Against Dion," *www.thecanadianpress.com,* May 29, 2007.

21. CTV.ca news staff, "Tory Ad Attacks Dion's Fiscal Imbalance Stance," April 2, 2007.

22. Joan Bryden, "Harper Predicts Personal Attacks; Ignores Demonization of Dion," *www.edmontonsun.com/News/Canada/2008/09/07/6693086.html*

23. Steve Maher, "Keeping Grit Voters Home Works for Harper," Halifax *Chronicle Herald,* October 18, 2008.

24. Stéphane Dion press conference, National Press Theatre, October 20, 2008. "I will do everything to make sure that my successor will be protected against this type of propaganda."

    "The image the Conservatives gave to me is cemented in the minds of too many Canadians, I want to protect the next leader against that." Video available: *www.cbc.ca/clips/mov/dion-announce081020.mov*

25. Douglas Todd, "Federal Conservative Attack Ads 'Poisoned' Election: TV Attacks On Liberal Leader Stéphane Dion Dissuaded Many Voters, Angus Reid Says," *Vancouver Sun,* October 24, 2008.

26. Maher, "Keeping Grit Voters Home."

27. Todd, "Federal Conservative Attack Ads 'Poisoned' Election."

28. Simon Doyle, "Prime Time Ad Blitz, Parties to Go Negative in Final 10 Days," *The Hill Times,* October 6, 2008.

CHAPTER 4

1. Howard Kurtz, *Media Circus: The Trouble with America's Newspapers* (New York: Times Books, 1994), p. 13.

2. David Taras, *Power and Betrayal in the Canadian Media* (Peterborough: Broadview Press, 2001), p. 1.

3. Senate of Canada, *Report of the Special Senate Committee on Mass Media, 1970*, p. 67.

4. Ibid., p. 71.

5. Maude Barlow and James Winter, *The Big Black Book: The Essential Views of Conrad and Barbara Amiel Black* (Toronto: Stoddart, 1997), p. 2.

6. Ibid., p. 40.

7. Canada, *Report of the Royal Commission on Newspapers, 1981*, p. 1.

8. Ibid., pp. 219-20.

9. Barlow and Winter, *The Big Black Book,* p. 23.

10. Ibid., p. 19.

11. "Canadian Media Who's Whose," *www.yourmedia.ca/library/whose.shtml*

12. Paul Palango, *Dispersing the Fog: Inside the Secret World of Ottawa and the RCMP* (Toronto: Key Porter, 2008), p. 402.

13. From Canwest MediaWorks Inc, PN 2006-5, p. 19, cited in the brief of the Canadian Media Guild to the CRTC, "The Most Media Diversity for the Most Canadians," re Broadcasting Notice of Public Hearing, CRTC 2007-5, July 18, 2007.

14. Senate of Canada, Standing Senate Committee on Transport and Communications, *Final Report on the Canadian News Media* (2006), vol. 2, p. 4.

15. Taras, *Power and Betrayal,* p. 173.

16. Senate of Canada, *Final Report on the Canadian News Media* (2006), vol. 1, p. 17.

17. Ibid., vol. 2, p. 5.

18. Taras, *Power and Betrayal,* p. 240.

19. Thomas Patterson, *Out of Order* (New York: Alfred A. Knopf, 1993), p. 92.

20. Paul Martin, *Hell or High Water: My Life In and Out of Politics* (Toronto: McClelland & Stewart, 2008), p. 449.

21. Ibid., p. 451.

22. Tony Burman, "The Election Debate Process Is a Sham," *Globe and Mail,* September 10, 2008.

23. Chantal Hébert, "Networks Have Lost Their Journalistic Backbone," *Toronto Star,* September 10, 2008.

24. Burman, "The Election Debate."
25. Steve Murphy's role in the decision to broadcast the tapes received a lot of press attention in Halifax and on some media blog sites. CTV's *W5* host, Jim Reed, condemned the decision of the network's hierarchy on his blog site *www.reedwrites.ca* on October 11, 2008. A longer account of the incident appears on the site of the Canadian Journalism Project (*www.j-source.ca*), in an article by Susan Newhook, a professor at King's College, Halifax.

CHAPTER 5

1. Paul Palango, *Dispersing the Fog: Inside the Secret World of Ottawa and the RCMP* (Toronto: Key Porter, 2008), p. 296.
2. Gary Mason, "Dead Man's MP Fears Challenging RCMP," *Globe and Mail,* May 11, 2006.
3. Petti Fong, "B.C. Mountie Cleared in Shooting Death," *Toronto Star,* November 30, 2007.
4. Karen Howlett, "Sorbara Talks 'Blindsided' Mounties," *Globe and Mail,* March 13, 2006.
5. Carol Goar, "Confidence in RCMP Shaken," *Toronto Star,* May 29, 2006.
6. Ibid.
7. Mason, "Dead Man's MP Fears Challenging RCMP."
8. Palango, *Dispersing the Fog,* p. 275.
9. CTV.ca news staff, "Layton Says MP Regrets Comments About the RCMP," *www.ctv.ca/news,* May 14, 2006.
10. David Hutton, "RCMP Pension Scandal: How to Stop the Rot," *The Hill Times,* Monday, April 30, 2007.
11. Paul Kennedy, *Chair-Initiated Complaint Regarding the Public Disclosure by the RCMP of its Criminal Investigation of the Possible Breach of Security Regarding the Taxation of Canadian Corporate Dividends and Income Trusts: Final Report,* March 31, 2008, Appendix A, letter of November 28, 2006. Available at *www.cpc-cpp.gc.ca/prr/rep/rev/chair-pre/taxation-fiscal-finrp-eng.aspx*
12. EKOS polling numbers, included as Appendix J to the *Final Report* of RCMP Commissioner Paul Kennedy, March 31, 2008.
13. Susan Delacourt, "RCMP Probes Are Playing into Hands of Opposition," *Toronto Star,* January 7, 2006.

14. Ibid.

15. Ibid.

16. *Hansard,* Question Period transcripts, September 24, 2006.

17. Palango, *Dispersing the Fog,* p. 179.

18. Ibid.

19. CBCNews.ca staff: "RCMP Commissioner Giuliano Zaccardelli," *www.cbc.ca/news/background/rcmp/zaccardelli.html,* December 6, 2006.

20. Rick Salutin, "Our Own Hanging Chads," *Globe and Mail,* December 8, 2006.

21. Don Martin, "Block Party? No Clear Explanation Why Tories Obstructed RCMP Whistle-Blowers," *National Post,* April 3, 2007.

22. Ibid.

23. Ibid.

24. Rick Salutin, "Not a Bang, But a Whimper," *Globe and Mail,* May 18, 2007.

25. Kady O'Malley, "Goodale Calls for Apology; Tories Decline," *www.macleans.ca,* February 15, 2007.

26. Ibid.

27. Jeffrey Simpson, "Election Fever? Recall How the Last One Turned on a Letter," *Globe and Mail,* February 16, 2007.

28. Paul Kennedy, *Final Report,* p. 5.

29. Ibid., p. 6.

30. Ibid.

31. Ibid., p. 7.

32. Ibid.

33. Ibid., p. 8.

34. Ibid.

35. James Travers, "Deafening Silence on RCMP Scandal," *Toronto Star,* April 3, 2008.

36. Ibid.

37. Paul Kennedy, *Final Report,* p. 8.

38. Daniel Leblanc, Bernier Questioned by RCMP, *Globe and Mail,* November 21, 2008.

39. Crawford Kilian, "Time to Disband the RCMP," *The Tyee,* thetyee.ca/Views/2007/11/19/DisbandRCMP/?, November 19, 2007.

CHAPTER 6

1. Brenda O'Neill, *Indifferent or Just Different? The Political and Civic Engagement of Young People in Canada* (Ottawa: Canadian Policy Research Networks, 2007).

2. Henry Milner, "Are Young Canadians Becoming Political Dropouts?: A Comparative Perspective," IRPP *Choices,* vol. 11, no. 3, June 2005.

3. James Joyner, "2008 Voter Turnout Same as 2004," *Outside the Beltway* online blogspot, *www.outsidethebeltway.com/archives/2008_voter_turnout_same_as_2004_/,* November 7, 2008.

4. Milner, "Are Young Canadians Becoming Political Dropouts?," p. 4.

5. Jon Pammett and Lawrence LeDuc, "Explaining Turnout Decline in Canadian Federal Elections: A Survey of Non-voters," Elections Canada, March 2003, p. 40.

6. Maria Gratschew, "Compulsory Voting," International Institute of Democracy and Electoral Assistance (IDEA) website, *www.idea.int/vt/compulsory_voting.cfm,* April 2001.

7. Greg Barnes, "Compulsory Voting Means Ignoring Election Day Is Not an Option," *Seattle Times,* November 24, 2004.

8. Pammett and LeDuc, "Explaining Turnout Decline in Canadian Federal Elections," p. 48.

9. Henry Milner, "Are Young Canadians Becoming Political Dropouts?," p. 7.

10. Canadian Press article, December 14, 2008 citing Dominion Institute poll, December 9–12, 2008. Available at *www.cbc.ca/canada/story/2008/12/14/canada-survey.html.*

11. Pammett and LeDuc, "Explaining Turnout Decline in Canadian Federal Elections, p. 2.

12. Pippa Norris, *Young People and Political Activism: From the Politics of Loyalties to the Politics of Choice?* Report for the Council of Europe Symposium. November 27-28, 2003. Cited in Brenda O'Neill, "Indifferent or Just Different?"

13. Anne Milan, "Willing to Participate: Political Engagement of Young Adults," *Canadian Social Trends,* Statistics Canada, Winter 2005, Catalogue no. 11-008., p.6.

14. Milner, "Are Young Canadians Becoming Political Dropouts?," p. 3.

15. Ibid., p. 4.

16. 2002 National Geographic–Roper Global Geographic Literacy Survey, cited in Milner, p. 7.

17. Russell, *Two Cheers for Minority Government,* pp. 165-66.

18. Milner "Are Young Canadians Becoming Political Dropouts?," p. 11.

19. World Association of Newspapers survey, cited in Milner, p. 11.

20. Anne Milan, "Willing to Participate," p. 3.

21. *www.apathyisboring.ca*

22. Preston Manning speaking to Democracy 250 event at North Nova High School, New Glasgow, sponsored by the Pictou Antigonish Regional Library, May 22, 2008. From my notes.

23. CBCNews.ca staff, "Alliance Leader Lashes Out at Elections Canada," *www.cbc.ca/canada/story/2002/04/18/harper_workers020318.html,* April 18, 2002.

24. Bea Vongdouangchanh, "Kingsley Resignation Surprises MPs in Likely Election Year," *The Hill Times,* January 8, 2007.

25. Lise Richard, "Youth Voter Experience, St Francis Xavier University, Federal Election 2008," prepared for Central Nova Green Party.

26. Stephen Maher, "Keeping Grit Voters Home Works for Harper," Halifax *Chronicle-Herald,* October 24, 2008.

CHAPTER 7

1. Personal communications. John Fraser and Jim Fulton are the kind of politicians who make you believe politics can be a noble calling. Fulton left us, far too early, just before Christmas 2008.

2. Andrew Mayeda and Jack Aubry, "Lobbying Alive and Well in Ottawa," *Edmonton Journal,* January 21, 2008.

3. Daniel Leblanc, "Tories Break Promise on Lobbying: Draft Law Fails to Require Ministers to Register All Communication," *Globe and Mail,* January 5, 2008.

4. Mayeda and Aubry, "Lobbying Alive and Well in Ottawa."

5. Non-Smokers' Rights Association, "Tobacco Industry Front Groups in Canada," January 27, 2003. Available at *www.nsra-adnf.ca/cms/index.cfm?group_id=1222.*

6. Mayeda and Aubry, "Lobbying Alive and Well in Ottawa."

7. Hill & Knowlton website.

8. Democracy Watch, "Federal Conservatives' So-Called 'Federal Accountability Act' and Related Decisions Earn a D Grade for Only Partially Increasing Government Democracy and Accountability," news release, Friday, December 12, 2008.

9. Sharon Beder and Richard Gosden, "WPP, World Propaganda Power," PR Watch newsletter, vol. 8, no. 2, 2001. Available at *www.prwatch.org/prwissues/2001Q2/wpp.html*

10. From my notes taken while attending Prof. Melchin's class.

11. Democracy Watch, "Donations and Lobbying by Top Federal Government Contractors Reveal Problem of Money in Politics," news release, Thursday, October 31, 2002.

12. Jean-Pierre Kingsley, Speech to the International Political Science Association International Symposium, "Democracy and Political Party Financing," Montreal, May 8, 2003.

13. CTVNews, "Ex-Tory candidate Slams Party for Media Restrictions, November 4, 2007.

14. CBC News, "Another Conservative Attacks the In-Out Ad Scheme," April 25, 2008.

15. Pierre Lortie, *Report of the Royal Commission on Electoral Reform and Party Financing,* 1991, p. 324.

16. Kingsley, Speech to the International Political Science Association.

17. Russell, *Two Cheers for Minority Government* (Toronto: Emond Montgomery, 2008), p. 139.

18. Jamie Carroll, "Recession Provides Cover for Tory Attack," *Toronto Star,* November 29, 2008.

CHAPTER 8

1. Peter Russell, *Two Cheers for Minority Government* (Toronto, Emond Montgomery, 2008).

2. Eugene Forsey, "The Problem of 'Minority' Government in Canada," *Canadian Journal of Economics and Political Science* 30 (1964): 1-11, at p. 4.

3. Fair Vote Canada press release, "Electoral Dysfunction Once Again," October 15, 2008.

4. Angus Reid Strategies press release, "Almost Half of Canadians Open to Proportional Representation," December 11, 2008.

5. Patrick Boyer, in Foreword to Nick Loenen, *Citizenship and Democracy: A Case for Proportional Representation,* (Toronto: Dundurn Press, 1997), p.15.

6. Ibid.

7. John Wallace, "Reflections on the Constitutional and Other Issues Concerning Our Electoral System: The Past and the Future," *Victoria University of Wellington Law Review,* 2002, vol. 33, no. 3 and 4. Available at *www.austlii.edu.au/nz/journals/VUWLRev/2002/30.html.*

8. Ibid.

9. Ibid.

10. Loenen, *Citizenship and Democracy,* pp.124-26.

11. Lee Greenberg, "Province Blamed For Ignorance on Electoral Referendum" *Ottawa Citizen,* October 4, 2007.

12. Ibid.

13. Angus Reid Strategies press release, "Almost Half of Canadians Open to Proportional Representation."

CHAPTER 9

1. Brian Laghi and Steve Chase, "Facing a Crisis, Harper Instructs MPs to Be Less Confrontational," *Globe and Mail,* November 19, 2008.

2. Ibid.

3. Tom Flanagan, "Grits Won't Die – They'll Just Fade Away," *Globe and Mail,* August 28, 2008.

4. Jeffrey Simpson, "Economist with a tin heart, politician with a tin ear," *Globe and Mail,* November 28, 2008.

5. Don Martin, "Harper Has No One to Blame But Himself," *National Post,* November 28, 2008.

6. Kady O'Malley blog, "Updated: A Trip Down Minority Government Memory Lane," *www.macleans.ca,* November 28, 2008.

7. Ibid.

8. CBC News, "Jean's Decision Sets 'Very Dangerous' Precedent: Constitutional Law Expert," *www.cbc.ca/canada/story/2008/12/04/constitution-expert.html,* December 4, 2008.

9. CTV.ca News Staff, "Liberals Put New Limits on Opposition Motions," *www.ctv.ca/servlet/ArticleNews/story/CTVNews/1113873239909_20/?hub=TopStories,* Apr. 19 2005.

10. Lawrence Martin, "The G-G needs to break her queenly silence and explain herself," *Globe and Mail,* December 22, 2008.

11. Colin Perkel, "D'Oh Canada!" *Globe and Mail,* December 14, 2008.

12. Ronald Wright, letter to the editor, *Globe and Mail,* December 8, 2008.

13. CBC News, "Jean's Decision Sets 'Very Dangerous' Precedent."

14. Quoted in L. Martin, "The G-G Needs to Break Her Queenly Silence and Explain Herself," *Globe and Mail,* December 22, 2008

15. Peter Russell, *Two Cheers for Minority Government* (Toronto: Emond Montgomery, 2008), p. 167.

16. Ibid., p. 101.

17. Petra Kelly, "Towards a Green Europe, Towards a Green World," Closing Speech at the International Green Congress, Stockholm, Sweden, August 30, 1987.

18. Cited in Russell, *Two Cheers for Minority Government,* p. 153.

19. Ibid., p. 35.

20. L. Martin, "The G-G Needs to Break Her Queenly Silence and Explain Herself," *Globe and Mail,* December 22, 2008.

21. Kim Elliott, interview with Naomi Klein, "We Can't Lose This Moment," *Rabble.ca,* December 3, 2008

Index